Make

Hockey

Great Again

Make Hockey Great Again

Praise for MAKING HOCKEY GREAT AGAIN

Every Canadian involved in hockey needs to read this book. Mike opens the door and unlocks the pathway to improved hockey performance. This is a must read on your road to better hockey development.

Ken Hitchcock, NHL Coach, Team Canada Coach and Mentor

Playing the game for my entire life and now broadcasting, I have seen a lot of change in the game. Mike takes a science driven look at what we have been doing and what we can do to move the game of hockey development much further ahead. A revealing read.

Kelly Hrudey, NHL Goaltender, Lead Broadcaster at Hockey Night in Canada

When you apply the principles of Make Hockey Great Again - your road to becoming "the best you can be" becomes a reality. The book is an excellent window into how hard great players work and how they become dedicated to getting better every day.

Glenn Carnegie, Skills Coach for Vancouver Canucks

Hockey is an incredible game. It took me from my rink in my backyard in a small town in Saskatchewan to the Molson Center in Montreal. Michael's book is about how to become elite, not just in hockey, but elite in your chosen field of passion. The book has insights that reinforced what I thought, other ideas challenged me, but in the end it made me a better coach. When you "choose" to be great, the door is open. Players like, Tanev, Burrows and Dorsett who weren't drafted, but applied tireless work ethic together with their extraordinary ability to get back up and never quit.

Willie Desjardin, NHL Head Coach

Cutting edge principles that lead athletes and coaches down the road to long term success. Every hockey player and coach should own a copy of this book.

Dane Jackson, University of North Dakota Coach and longtime pal.

Simple and Powerful. Effective principles that are aimed to reward athletes and coaches that desire to be the best.

Jimmy McGroarty, USHL Head Coach and amazing coach at Total Package Hockey.

Mike shares with us the importance of self-determination and perseverance and why being talented is not nearly enough. Players, coaches and parents will learn effective strategies that unlock the pathway to excellence.

Chris Joseph, NHL Player and Youth Hockey Skills Coach Edmonton

Make Hockey Great Again

Copyright © 2018 by Mike Kennedy

www.GoldStandardHockey.com
All rights reserved. This book or any portion thereof may not be reproduced or used in any manner whatsoever without the express written permission of the publisher except for the use of brief quotations in a book review.

Printed in the United States of America

First Printing, 2018

ISBN 978-0-692-16553-9

www.goldstandardhockey.com

and;

www.makehockeygreatagain.com

Make Hockey Great Again

To My Mom, who I miss dearly, she would be so proud…

To My Dad, who let me go after my dreams, even when chasing dreams may not have been the most prudent thing to do. (Dad also helped organize my thoughts so this book would flow a lot better!)

And…

To my wife who supported me EVERY step of this incredible life journey. 23 years since we met in Dallas, I love you babe!

And finally, to my Aunt Sandra (Lovering) who provided the nuances to grammar and kept my eye on the prize.

Make Hockey Great Again

ABOUT THE AUTHOR IX

INTRODUCTION XIX

CHAPTER 1 3

HOCKEY SHIFT – PLAY AND COACH IN THE 21ST CENTURY 3

    1. Examine Current Limitations 7
    2. Use Reflective Thinking – to move forward 17
    3. Begin the Paradigm Shift - Innovation 24
    C. Things to consider when adopting small area games: 31
    D. Enhance – small area game competition 34
    E. Excellent - Practice Expectations 35

CHAPTER 2 39

WHAT MAKES MCDAVID AND MATTHEWS SO GOOD? 39

    Skill Progress 50
    Four ~~BASIC~~ COMPLEX Skills that need constant improvement 51
    Advanced skill building 67
    What it takes – Mental Toughness 69
    Multi-sport athletes 71
    Teaching? Coaching? Maybe we should adopt the term ->
    "Teachers." 73

CHAPTER 3 77

COACHING SECRETS 77

    COACHING SECRET #1: SEASON BREAKDOWN 79
    COACHING SECRET #2: GAME SITUATIONS 82
    COACHING SECRET #3: PLAYER POSITIONS 88
    COACHING SECRET #4: INNOVATION 97
    10 SECRETS OF AN   INCREDIBLE COACH 103
    COACHING SECRET #5: COACH & PLAYER RELATIONSHIP 106
    COACHING SECRET #6: PRACTICE 108
    COACHING SECRET #7: PREPARATION 129
        Head Coach Job Description 132
        Season Plan 137
        Block Plans 139
        Player Evaluation Meetings 147
        Player and Parent Feedback 148

CHAPTER 4 151

WINNING PARENTS	**151**
CHAPTER 5	**167**
PLAYERS – MAZIMIZE YOUR POTENTIAL	**167**
THREE stages of a youth hockey player's career	169
What are the best ways to get better?	172
CHAPTER 6	**191**
CHAMPION GOAL SETTING	**191**
Short-Term Goals	194
Medium Term Goals	194
Team Goals	194
Goal Setting: It's All in the Process	195
Process Goals	196
Performance Goals	197
Outcome Goals	197
Evaluate your Goals	200
CHAPTER 7	**203**
THE GAME IS CHANGING – MOSTLY FOR DEFENSEMAN	**203**
New age Defending	204
Skating	206
Back to youth hockey	208
Creating offense from Defense	209
Group of FIVE – how to score 5 on 5 goals	211
Defending has changed too	212
Defense – wins championships?	214
Coaches are once again beginning to focus on offense	217
CHAPTER 8	**219**
PRACTICE…WE TALKIN 'BOUT PRACTICE MAN?	**219**
Let's first examine the teacher.	219
Now lets' look at the Peewee Coach	221
1. Season Plan	222
2. Block Plans	223
3. Practice Plans	225
Great Thoughts	228
Deliberate Practice	228
CHAPTER 9	**231**

THE REAL QUESTION IS…HOW? 231
    The Bottom Up and Top Down Approaches 232
    ALWAYS HAVE THE ATHLETES COGNITIVELY BE ENGAGED. 233
    Deliberate Practice 235

CHAPTER 10 239

THE TRUTH 239
    Part 1. Hockey is FUN. 240
    Part 2. Small Area Games – Development and FUN 240
    Part 3. TALENT IS OVERRATED. 243
    Part 4. Coaching. 246
    Part 5. Parenting Better 249
    Part 6. And Finally – New age Defense. 250
1. UPDATED HOCKEY SKILL SETS 254
   1. Puckhandling – tied to VISION 255
   2. Body Checking – New School 257
   3. Shooting – The wrister is KING 258
   4. Passing – Old vs New School 261
   5. Cycling – 80's vs today's game 262
   6. Backchecking (now called "Tracking," a Ken Hitchcock term) 263
   7. Offensive Zone Entry – Let's get CREATIVE 265
   8. Conditioning – get it done DURING practice 267
   9. Skill Building 269
2. EFFECTIVE DECISION-MAKING 275
3. BEST CURRICULUM & CORE SKILLS 280
4. PLAYER - SELF EVALUATION 286
5. "ASSOCIATION" GREATNESS 289
6. "EXECUTIVE" GREATNESS 298

About the Author

What's up hockey enthusiast! I am very happy that you are going to take a journey with me on how we can make hockey great again!

My name is Mike Kennedy and my journey down the road of writing and publishing my first book (never know, there might be more) has been immensely enjoyable. As a former NHL player of 145 games and a whole lot of healthy scratches, I became inspired to learn more about coaching and how we can do things better. As my 6 year old son took off dragging his right foot along behind him for what seemed like a whole year, I was determined to find a fresh, innovative way to coach and train youth hockey players. My journey to learn more was set in motion in 2006.

I wanted this book to be authentic. Raw. In my only year of University, I failed English. The final exam was to write an essay on any number of topics. I thought I nailed it. Wrong. But that didn't stop me from writing this book. Failure – it's not an obstacle, it's a hurdle. I want to thank my only two editors – my dad and my aunt Sandra. Keep it raw. Keep it real. This is me and I want the world to know that you don't have to have an English degree (or even pass English 101) to get your message out!

This book is already a best seller. My family loves it. And they didn't even buy a copy. Freebies for family I guess. The research, the passion, the dedication to seeing this project through speak of a testament to self-determination. No publisher. No ghost writer. No Formatter. No Publicist. Just me and a lot of YouTube training. I am Self-published and proud to be able to help many coaches, parents and players around the globe who are driven to learn the secrets of becoming your best!

My journey from house league to the big league is what a reasonable person might call – crazy. But it always begins with an unwavering determination to improve. I played my minor hockey in and around Toronto. From the ages of 7-9 years old I played for a "C" town in Tottenham (not AAA!), a great little town 45 minutes north west of Toronto. When our family moved back to Toronto, my mom searched out the top program and next thing you know, I had been invited to tryout with the Toronto Marlboros for my Peewee year. I only played one year with the most famous minor hockey team in the country. FOUR players on the Marlie peewee team played at least 1 game in the NHL. 1 player is in the Hockey Hall of Fame. Eric Lindros, Drake Berehowsky, Mike Torchia and I all played in the NHL. And I remember hearing at that time that the chances of making it to the NHL were almost zilch. Well, we proved whoever said that to be dead wrong. We had a great season, but my mom hated all the driving that was required of playing for this impressive team, although I loved the 6am Saturday morning practices at Maple Leaf Gardens and attending the matinee Jr. A Marlie game after a long brunch. From Bantam to Midget I played with the much closer Mississauga Reps and for a great coach – Mr. Rick Moretta.

I did not have any skills coaches, skating coaches or dryland coaches. But I did have one significant advantage – tons and tons of ice time. And Mr. Moretta kept us in shape; he loved the "one mile skate," which is 16 laps to be completed for the last 5 minutes of many practices. Seems pretty easy – but try it, It was a killer! I played high school hockey for Michael Power, club hockey for the Reps, and I played outdoor hockey (free) almost every chance I could get. Swerving around kids younger than you, trying to puck protect against older kids. It was total freedom. If Malcolm Gladwell / Anders Ericsson say you need 10,000 hours to master a sport, I was WAY ahead of the pack vs all the kids in my age group. Not to mention the countless hours of ball hockey in my driveway. I have been asked, "how did you MAKE the NHL?" to which I usually respond, "I hold the Canadian record for most hours playing street hockey." My obsession was in motion and I truly spent almost every free second I had at home with my hockey net a tennis ball and a few neighbours!

To become a world class athlete, players need to become self-motivated and self-determined. Setbacks and struggle have to form part of the journey. And for me, my first major setback happened during my grade 11 year, when my mom and step dad moved to Vancouver at Christmas time. My mom was sick with breast cancer, and I knew that staying in Toronto was not an option. I played the rest of the season on a team of washed up 20-year-olds who preferred beer to hockey. My second setback happened next. After my mom passed away from breast cancer in the spring of my grade 11 year, I knew I needed to go somewhere where hockey could be a more significant part of my life. My dad found a school that he thought fit the bill, so I enrolled at Notre Dame, a high school in Saskatchewan that specialized in developing young hockey players. I expected to be close to making the Jr. A team, but didn't even make the AAA Midget team, falling down to the AA level as a 17-year-old midget player. So much for an NCAA scholarship. I was devastated. I was pissed. And I took it out on my new school.

I did however get good enough grades to be accepted into one of the most prestigious Universities in Canada – University of British Columbia. Once on campus, I learned that the Varsity team's tryouts were upcoming. Never afraid of another failure, I went to the tryouts. I was shocked to learn that the returning players were all aged between 21-24 and that every one of them had played in the WHL (Western Hockey

League) for a number of seasons. As a skinny 18-year-old, 6'1 and 165 pounds and not one single Jr. game played under my belt, I was determined to give it my best shot. Tryouts went well because I was paired with a couple veteran players and as tryouts concluded, coach Terry O'Malley named me to the team. Finally! Something good was happening.

The season was remarkable, a breakthrough and one of the most memorable seasons of my career. A great group of players and role models. They collectively helped me to be my best, and it began to show. As the season turned towards the second half, the pay phone on my dorm's floor began to ring. I would hear a scream coming from down the hall, "Hey Kennedy, Quebec Nordiques are on the phone!!" and I would run to grab the phone and shut the phone booth style door to chat with a scout for a few minutes. The NHL is calling? – I must be dreaming.

I was selected 97th overall by the Minnesota North Stars who the next year moved to Dallas, and I quickly realized that I needed to start training like a pro.

Following my year at UBC, I enjoyed my only year in junior as a 19-year-old, serving my second of three straight rookie years. Loading the bus and all the nonsense that the rookies do, the leading scorer of the Seattle Thunderbirds was no different, and I was happy to oblige. Part of the reason I picked Seattle was that they were hosting the Memorial Cup – what a thrill to play in such a prestigious tournament. The other reason I picked Seattle was that my girlfriend was only a two hour drive north, back in Vancouver.

In Seattle, we were coached extremely well by Peter Anholt, but we couldn't string the wins together. Even though we started the first half of the year 10 games under .500, we pulled off a couple trades, got Chris Osgood in net and made a great run to the end of the season, won two playoff rounds and lost in the Conference Finals to eventual Memorial Cup Winner and powerhouse, Kamloops Blazers. It was a great experience to be treated as a pro and I was thirsty for more.

As a 20-year-old, I began the professional journey of climbing my way out of the minor leagues. The competition was tough with 2nd rounders, 3rd rounders, 4th rounders from prior years and my year and soon to be following years. The competition only grew in Kalamazoo, Michigan. As a 5th rounder, you sometimes begin to think, will I ever make it out of here? I have to figure out which player on the Stars that I think I can replace. My time was coming.

My starting minor league salary - $27,500. Not bad for a 20-year-old is what I thought. (NHL salary was a whopping $160,000)

And then Ken Hitchcock arrives in my sophomore year. And things really change. Details were put in place. Accountability to play hard every night was instilled. And Ken's reliance on veteran players added up to reduced ice time and some healthy scratches scattered across a year in which I wish I could have forgotten. What the F? In my exit interview after my second season, I looked Ken straight in the eye and told him, "next year, I am going to be your GO TO guy" and his response was – "that is exactly what I wanted to hear."

Make Hockey Great Again

The following year was the lockout of '95, and most NHL players were headed to Europe because of the lockout, but the minor leaguers were not locked out and our season began on time. As the season wore on and the Christmas break came and went, I was praying for an Agreement – I was leading the team in scoring by a wide margin, and it looked promising to be called up to the BIG team if the season could just get underway.

Yes! Lockout concluded. Only a short NHL training camp in mid-January and the season would be underway. And I proved that I had earned a roster spot on the team! Wow, could anything be better than this? Yes, it could. Our first game of the season was in Vancouver, my home at UBC and all my 4th year graduating pals would be watching! My dad flew out to the game. Goose bumps everywhere. And a pass from behind the net to the edge of the crease to my line mate, Paul Broten who smartly deflected the pass my way to the other side of the crease and I also one touched the pass (a nifty slider under goalie, Kirk Mclean) – I was the leading scorer for the Dallas Stars for a brief period in time! The game ended 1-1 and our team headed to Whistler for some more training camp days and a rookie party dinner that cost me 10% off my salary from that season. Thanks, Araxi. That night is another book!

As I look back on my career, I am proud of how far I got and how resilient to struggle I became. I was motivated and became better than I thought possible. What is truly amazing is that I did this all by myself. I don't think this is possible anymore. And, looking back, I wish I had some skills coaches that could have helped me with the subtler points of becoming an effective scorer at the highest level. Concentrating on skills where TIME is squeezed – I often felt like I had absolutely ZERO time to make smart plays.

However, now as I look at how my career unfolded and I see elite youth players receiving NHL like coaching at an early age, I am convinced that this book will help every player who aspires to become their best.

Part II - NOW

It would be deceptive if I were to write this book and not to adopt the principles herein.

The date today is Oct 24, 2018 and I am excited. I recently spoke with Ken Hitchcock and Kelly Hrudey. The final piece of the book is coming together, namely the praise for the front/back of the book.

Before I spoke to Kelly, I made sure to read his book titled, Calling the Shots. And one chapter really spoke to me – Chapter 15, I'm the Worst Goalie in the League. Resolve. Persistence and Character brought Kelly out of this funk – along with a little help from Tony Robbins. On page 164, Kelly talks about a movie in which a documentary team films one of Tony's best 6 day seminars, the movie is called *I'm Not Your Guru*. Naturally I had to watch it. And after watching it – I figure I would put my goals in print - here goes:

Mike Kennedy – Mission Statement

To be unstoppable in my quest to become an NHL coach. A great coach has the exact same qualities needed to be a great player – it takes an incredible amount of work ethic, hunger, persistence, grit and a competitive thirst to get better every day. I am hungry to get better at coaching every day.

Immediate Goal

To help a high level (Jr. Hockey and beyond) team achieve competitive greatness and win a league championship. By effectively using emotional intelligence, I want to inspire players to reach their own goals.

3 year Goal

To be at the helm of a high level team. And to influence the next biggest advantage – the "ENVIRONMENT" in which we as coaches and athletes train to get better. To have other high level coaches ask, "what is he doing?" that makes his teams so successful.

The previous two advantages are now a much smaller advantage than only a few years ago. (The Analytics teams have flattened the benefit of analytics and the importance of character of each teammate will soon be compressed to very little value – read The Cubs Way, the Zen of Building the Best Team in Baseball. Although many NHL and Jr. teams still struggle putting the right character together in one group.)

5-10 year Goal

To coach hockey at the HIGHEST level. The NHL. Boom, I said it.

My feeling is that in the next 10 years, fans will have a very hard time deciphering who is a forward and who is a defenseman. Teams that embrace an attack without any trepidation of a forward playing defense for the remainder of a shift will continue to reap the rewards of challenging for the Stanley Cup.

Watch 3 on 3 overtime and you see the most exciting part of the game. Teams will slowly advance their 5 on 5 offense to simulate the current 3 on 3 style we see now. Man on man coverage, creating confusion with scissor and screen plays are now common place in the NHL. Jr and youth hockey still have a long ways to go to embrace these philosophies.

Imagine being on offense and taking the puck out of the offensive zone ON PURPOSE! Wow, we might be a ways away from that happening, but there are definite indications that this play will form part of the next generation of player's skill sets.

Hockey will keep evolving and my job is to be on the cusp of the leading edge.

Introduction

This book is about achieving – MORE. It is for parents, players, and coaches. Here is perhaps the most critical key: persistence.

Accept full responsibility for your own future. And it starts with an attitude. One that says, I am here to get better. And every second is counted towards achieving more. For coaches and players - Are you committed to continually improve? This book will be the first, and hopefully not last of adopting a keep moving forward principle.

When I set out to write this book, I had one thing in my mind – can we do this better? If the number of hours of training is fixed, the question becomes how can we increase the quality of the training? And included in the way we train young hockey players is that it must be enjoyable!

Fun? What the heck. Fun needs a definition here, and for an aspiring young hockey player, here is the definition: To be constantly challenged in a competitive manner.

The shocking piece of what I discovered is that sports always make sense. Steps are taken. First this, then this.

Technical skills are broken down and taught. The sequence becomes important.

And so, you have to ask the question (as more and more kids are doing) – why are we doing this? Then we have to look for the answer. And from what I found out, this was the typical answer from a coach – "because that is what we have always done." Time to change this attitude.

Time for an updated approach to the dinosaur techniques that I still see at every rink across North America. This book generates a new way of approaching development. Speaking of development – this word is so overused and it disturbs me how many different ways that development is defined by. This book will dive deeply into development, for coaches, players, and parents.

The book starts off by taking a longer look at what we currently have been doing and tries to strip away conventional practicing and replace it with deep practice explained in depth – soon!

There are an inadequate number of hockey books that delve into how to train for performance. The research is out there for sport in general, and because soccer is a global game, it is a leader in development with the thousands of Academies across the Globe promoting their science-driven paths to develop stars for their Club and National teams.

Note: If you want top-notch, cutting edge hockey development, the NHL should abandon the draft. Each team should be responsible for developing their OWN players. Wow. That would be incredible. However, it is not going to happen.

So, we move on and learn from the best soccer academies in the world and learn from some Elite Athletes like Connor McDavid and Austin Matthews.

When researching this book, I read more than 100 books, hundreds of articles and countless google searches during my pursuit to find a better way. And what I found was that all arrows of science land on the same target -> <u>practice must be designed to be VERY similar to a game.</u> Outcomes may be varied, but coaches must learn to place their players on the edge of their abilities with decision-making skills forming the most significant component of each drill.

Hockey endures a turnover every 2 seconds. 400+ in an NHL game. Hmmmm…yet most coaches want our practices to be perfect, with coaches adjusting timing, passing drills are scripted, shooting pucks without confrontation and players behaving like robots. Seems exactly the opposite of a game to me.

To find out what other elite performers were doing, I looked at the tactical team games – from English Field Hockey to Soccer and Football. How are the top end coaches adopting principles that enhance the player's performance while keeping the training exciting?

I looked at motivation, why are some players extremely motivated. Hint: Early success forms a big part…Setting and achieving goals and learning the secrets to grit. Learning how to never give up, embrace the biggest challenges and to see failure as a pathway to success. Blah, Blah, Blah. Seen it before, but get ready for this ride, it is worth it.

I tackle the secrets that make Connor McDavid and Auston Matthews so good. Hint: Small area games and constant opposition to the skill being mastered. To let another secret out of the bag – they both played a lot of hockey and both had NHL level skills coaches for most of their youth hockey! This of course comes at a price, sport specific development – what about the multi-sport approach that we hear being preached to us nonstop?

I looked at coaching secrets that are often overlooked and must be more closely scrutinized.

Skills, Skills, Skills – yes, but in the right environment. If not, they are a waste of time. I spend time discussing the state of the positions in the game and how to maximize player position development.

Goal setting and responsible ownership of each player's future is tackled.

Areas of the game's most noticeable changes are detailed and what coaches and players can do to keep up with this evolving transition.

Make Hockey Great Again

The difficulty lies not in developing new ideas but escaping old ones.

-John Maynard Keynes

Chapter 1

Hockey shift – play and coach in the 21st Century

Sport scientists on the cutting edge are constantly redefining the accepted theories on optimal athletic training. In reaction to both scientific and common-sense realizations, many sports now contain practice routines that look vastly different from what they looked like twenty years ago. Hockey, however, has changed VERY little.

Paradigm is defined as: an outstandingly clear example showing how something is to be done. Then what is the current North American hockey practice paradigm? In watching hundreds of hockey practices every year, I am amazed at the similarities most practices contain. Here is what I see:

- A slow-moving warm-up that typically includes stretching muscles while sitting or lying on the ice.

- Skating drills that are not specific to game situations or designed to build and improve technique.
- A few flow drills such as 2 on 0's or 3 on 0's which ypically result in players skating at much slower speeds than they would in a game situation and make passes and take shots that would not be an option in actual competition.
- Coaches spending very expensive minutes at a hockey board explaining drills, but rarely if ever explaining the purpose of the drill without ever teaching the skill.
- A number of different team drills, such as 5 on 0 breakouts, which consume a great deal of time and don't allow for the number of quality repetitions players need to fully develop a skill or grasp a concept.
- Practices finishing with traditional conditioning drills such as lightning drills or skating wallys (across the ice – back and forth). Even though we are supposed to be training for a sport that requires quick bursts of power and energy.

Does any of this look familiar to you? As a coach, do you see practices that are run like this? Do you run your practices like this?

The current paradigm is outdated. Twenty and thirty years ago, players could overcome the type of practice routine outlined above by developing their skills on the pond or the outdoor rink.

Outdoor rinks would be crowded with kids of all ages, developing and honing their skills while playing the game and having fun. No adults to organize and criticize. No whistles, no talk, no overzealous parents screaming from the stands. Society has changed and hockey has changed along with it. There is too much structure and too many other options to occupy youth hockey player's time.

Every day coaches in our country have conversations lamenting these facts and longing for the good old days, wishing things would return to the way they were. But we all know that things are not going to go back to the way they were. Rather than giving in to this realization and deciding that there just isn't anything we as coaches can do about it, I would argue that we need to be more creative with our practice time. It is up to us to help our players learn the skills and hockey sense that once came naturally from time spent on the outdoor rinks.

These ideas and methods of teaching are simply known as "old school." Still today, a large part of how I see hockey coaches teaching our youth – they are using the same drills and teaching points that have been around since the 1970's. For example: When I watch a team perform the horseshoe before every game is like taking a high stick to the chin.

The other powerful connection to distinguish between the old school and today is COST. Hockey is becoming increasingly expensive and it is critical to get the MOST out of a 60 minute practice where ice can cost up to $7/minute or more. Thoughtless planning, lousy organization, poor management, too much coach talk, too many minutes standing at a hockey board, stretching on the ice all form a colossal waste of time and leads to a miserable experience for everyone involved.

Imagination is the origin of wisdom.

We need to get hockey out from the time warp. Can we stop for a minute and actually see what is going on around us? It seems too many coaches are blind to the practice plans and pre-game warmups. What I mean is: What purpose does the horseshoe serve? 14 players standing around, 1 player skating. Seems like a no-brainer to toss this drill in the garbage, yet I see it EVERY day.

So we must use our imagination to find more meaning in the way we train our players. Can we use "reflective" thinking to change the way we train our youth? What works? What doesn't? What technology can we use? What teaching plan? A curriculum imposed? What are the worthwhile alternatives to traditional teaching methods? Can this book help you as a coach to break free of the old school methods and adopt new ideas that actually make learning the game a lot MORE fun?

So, in order to be clear here, there are 3 areas we must address when looking at hockey development:

1. Examine current limitations

2. Use Reflective Thinking
3. Begin the Paradigm Shift - Innovation

Coaches must first examine the limitations of traditional training methods. Then through reflection, associations can outline the detail of advantages, key concepts, conceptual framework, and innovative approach to teaching hockey.

To "experiment" means that you do something, you manipulate, you change something in a systematic way under controlled conditions in order to discover something. This book is about moving hockey coaches and players forward and discovering new ideas to the way we train youth hockey players.

1. Examine Current Limitations

I am in hockey rinks almost every day and often in different parts of the country. I get excited when I see something 'new.' Unfortunately, this is a rarity. As a group of coaches, my hope is that we constantly push the envelope and continually find new and improved methods to the way we teach hockey.

The areas of immediate attention for examining the CURRENT LIMITATIONS include:

    A. Isolation learning
    B. Recycled Drills
    C. Strategy / Systems are BOTH Problematic
    D. Lack of Skill Building scenarios

A. Isolation Learning

Skills are often taught in isolation rather than as part of the natural context of executing strategy in game-like situations and must be reworked to be taught in a non-conventional way. The value of the exercise must be taught in a way that players can experience the game feel in practical application.

A coach skating his team around circles and cones must be stopped dead in his tracks. If there is a core skill that is being worked on, like outside edges, or crossovers – try to find a game situation that will help improve the skill.

Learning drills that have no game feel to the player is like racing your bike with training wheels on. It actually hurts to have those damn wheels on the bike. Isolation learning is the kryptonite to hockey development; small area games are the antidote. More on small area games later.

B. Recycled Drills

I continue to see the same drills that I performed as a youth player at every rink I go to. Recycled mostly because coaches don't know where to look to get new, innovative drills that put athletes on the edge of their abilities. These drills are often combined with zero teaching points associated with them. Zero application to games. And even worse, sometimes these drills negatively affect skill development – which means that by performing this drill you actually get worse!

Make Hockey Great Again

Bantam   Length: 60 mins   Number of Players: 16-20

Equipment: x cones, x tires, x border pads, x nets

Drill Name: Team Canada

This drill is a robotic passing drill that is completely useless and forms many bad habits.

F1 – shoots the puck from the slot (never happens in a game) and does not stop in front or even try to get a rebound.
F1 – continues after shot to find a loose puck either behind net or in corner.
F2 – uses timing (this play would never happen in a game) to swoop in from top of circle on boards and cuts to the middle of the ice (usually turning back to the F1 player)
F2 - receives a 15-25 foot pass from F1

F3 – swoops from center ice to boards (usually turning back and losing sight of F2 if only momentarily.
F2 – relays puck to F3 (F2 – in drill for less than 3 seconds.)

F3 – attacks goalie, shoots puck from an area that never happens in a game and the drill continues.

Both ends go at the same time.

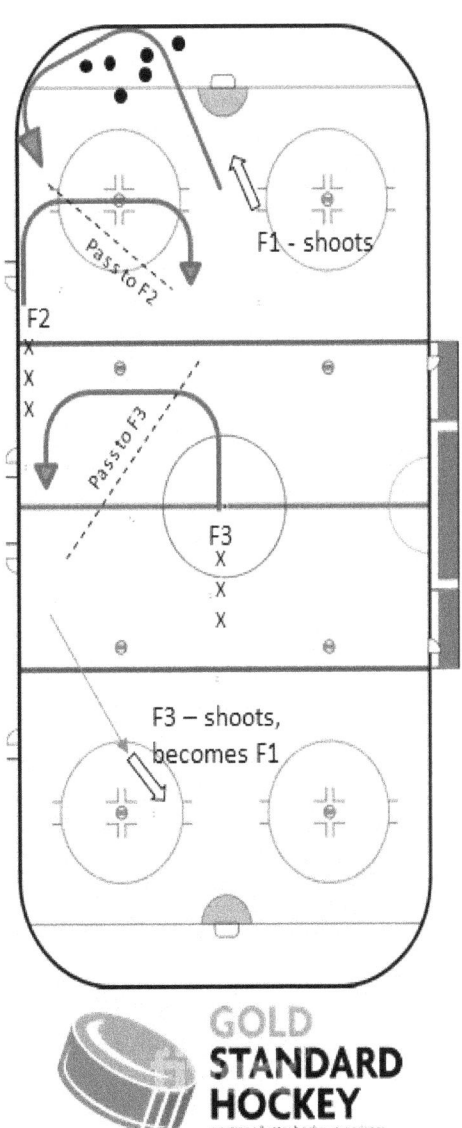

Want another one? Just ask yourself what your team does for the (three to five minute) warmup before the game. 90% of coaches put their team through the same meaningless and useless drill that has been unchanged since the 1970's. For the 10% of coaches that innovate a new, fresh way to get your team warmed up – congrats! I always watch a team warmup, and from this warmup I can tell if the team has an "old" school coach or not. In fact, when I interview coaching candidates I ask them to draw out their team on-ice warmup. Then I would ask, "why?" And guess what the answer is 99/100 – "because that is what has always been done." And this answer further reinforces the reason this book is so important.

Recycled drills are everywhere on the internet, but all of these drills feature one huge hockey development CURSE: the drill is actually a "script," a set of instructions, based on timing of teammates moving in a scripted fashion. The coach draws up on the hockey board, player 1 goes here, player 2 goes here, and player one passes to...you get the idea. These SCRIPTS do not have a lifespan of more than 2 seconds in a hockey game because a hockey game involves 5 opposing players trying their best to MESS your script up. Yet, somehow since the 1970's this approach to training continues to be at the core of how we teach hockey to youth players. These drills take away from the precious development of learning from "possibilities" and decision-making skills which form the core of developing hockey skills and sense. However, there is an antidote!

The best question a coach needs to think about when trying to decide whether to put a drill into the practice plan is this: what decisions are being made by my players? How can I influence the drill to have multiple outcomes? What if the drill breaks down perhaps by missed passes or poor execution – can the drill continue in the face of a potential break down? The answer lies in a game situation – what will happen in a game when a play recognized by the entire team fails...the game does not stop...the game continues on...and a new set of possibilities arise. In practice if the drill breaks down and the coach requires a "restart" the only part that breaks down is the player's ability to solve the next situation. I get it, we as coaches want to solve the PRESENT situation with skill and execution, but we rarely focus on what happens when the execution is NOT there and the skill fails – what now? This scenario happens every 5 seconds in a hockey game.

C. Strategy Development better known as: Systems – are problematic

The major problem in developing youth hockey players is a coach's continual desire to improve the team's strategic part of the game. An unnecessary, time consuming piece of hockey development revolves around strategy. The major reason that strategy continues to be a "main" focus for youth hockey coaches is because many youth hockey coaches do not possess the ability to teach skillful tactics. Teaching skillful plays has been replaced with teaching disciplined strategy. Examples of strategy include:

- Multiple breakout patterns
- Forecheck systems like 1-2-2, or 2-1-2 among others
- Neutral zone systems
- Defensive zone coverage assignments
- Powerplay systems including breakouts
- PK systems up ice and in zone

Every time a coach spends time on the above mentioned systems it will definitely help his team "win" more often. There is NO DOUBT about it. A team that plays a disciplined system will win a lot of games. The real issue with this is: at what COST? For every minute spent on the "System" that helps win hockey games, a minute is taken from developing a player's skill set needed to solve problems. The opportunity to teach player's skills has been lost.

The COST of winning is costing time which is better spent on improving a player's individual skill set. Hint: an individual skill set is the ability to use experience to solve problems and weave together multiple steps/plays in a time crunched environment. Therefore, it doesn't take too much to understand that spending considerable time teaching "Strategy Development/Systems" will actually hinder a player's ability to improve his/her own skill sets by way of reducing precious time in this area. Skill time is taken away from areas like: passing, puck protection, shooting and getting open to name a few of the thousands of skills young players need to learn?

Even worse, to employ STRATEGY successfully, coaches must impose strict parameters on players and their "responsibilities" on the ice. And, this takes tons and tons of TIME to teach players how to successfully enable strategy tactics. The word "disciplined" player comes to mind. This is a surefire way to hinder development.

First, in practice, coaches spend countless hours on perfecting strategy at the mercy of learning "skilled plays." Eating up development time, seconds ticking away.

Secondly, many coaches send the wrong message to young hockey players on how they must play "risk free." Continually preaching defense first and stay within the system are the death of a young hockey player. A player that gambles - hoping that a puck will squirt loose to the offensive side of a puck battle is scorned by many coaches and is replaced by teaching players to always error on the defensive side of the puck – in almost every situation. Yuck!

Because of the constant preaching of defense and system play, players are very often made afraid about failing their defensive responsibilities. Many youth hockey players have adopted an extremely limited risk approach to their game. Hockey is a risk/reward game, and an athlete's job is to constantly evaluate the risks and rewards.

A developing hockey player should not be afraid of making mistakes and miscalculating risk, instead they should be congratulated and encouraged to learn from each misread and success. My rule of thumb is that players should error on the side of caution in an equal proportion as the side of risk!

Sadly, many coaches misunderstand the statistics of how risky an outnumbered situation ACTUALLY can be. For example: The worst possible outnumbered situation is a breakaway, followed by a (2 on 1) rush. What are the typical scoring rates (goals) associated for these two situations that arose out of a player miscalculating a risk?

Let's take an example of a: Peewee AAA team. Coaches, I don't want to give you my data instead, I want you to perform your own statistical analysis – set up a 2 on 1 in practice, that is similar to a game, with a backchecker skating relentlessly from a position that is not TOO far away. Before you do your own analysis, take a guess at what the completion percentage will be. My analysis shows that it is LESS than 10%. Now you tell me, is this a risky situation? I have found that breakaways with a backchecker chasing the player down are often times successful at less than 10% as well, which puts breakaways in second place as most risky situations to give up. Hmmm...

To dig in a little bit, the risk continually climbs higher as athletes get older and their experience begins to come into play and better execution begins to win over. For example, the risk of giving up a 2 on 1 in Peewee is a lot less than it is in Junior hockey.

Unfortunately, many youth hockey coaches watch the NHL too often and confuse the risk of giving up an outnumbered rush to players earning millions of dollars with the same risk as a youth player. To assume that NHL players and youth hockey players have the same risk (likelihood of scoring a goal) is completely wrong – nothing could be further from the truth.

Coaches must ask themselves which scenario do you take more pride in:

> "I won 3 city championships, 1 provincial/state title and 12 tournaments over my 10 years as a Bantam coach." (If this is you, then keep working on systems and strategy)

OR

> "I helped develop 10 players who are now playing Jr or NCAA hockey." (If this is you, then keep working on skilled plays and decision-making abilities)

D. Lack of skill building scenarios

Most coaches underestimate the true complexity of developing a skill. Most coaches do not possess the ability to teach the finer points of complex skills and because of their inabilities they tend to swerve away from the details that are drastically important in refining a complex skill. Coaches who lack the ability to teach complex skills choose strategy over skill development. There is a way to curb this behavior. (keep reading)

Let's examine what a complex skill is? A complex skill is a skill that can be used to solve real problems in a SPLIT SECOND. So for a skill to be complex, the skill must be attached to limited time. I call limited time – game situation. The complexity is the speed at which the skill needs to be performed to have a positive outcome in a game situation.

Now let's examine the word - tactic. The definition of tactic is: "a planned action for a particular purpose." In hockey this definition gets a little boost – "planned actionS for a particular purpose." Tactics are multiple skillful plays that are weaved together for a purpose. Teaching the tactics of weaving together skillful plays is the PURPOSE of a coach.

A gifted coach will look at a drill and figure out a way to incorporate a "skilled play" into the drill. As players progress, coaches can utilize adding in skilled plays by presenting disturbances to the decision makers. Most often times, decision makers are the players that possess the puck, but equally as important are the decisions of each player moving about the ice WITHOUT the puck. Supporting the puck carrier, getting open, finding opportunities to accept passes all form decisions made away from the puck carrier.

An example of a drill that incorporates skillful play with decision making: a typical breakout involving putting a defenseman under pressure from a forechecker, the defenseman will need to learn to find the appropriate "escape" maneuver and execute it with improved timing. Perhaps on the way to the puck retrieval, the defenseman had to skate 3 hard backward strides and pivot. What are the details in a perfectly executed pivot? Figuring out the speed of the forechecker, considering throwing in a "deceptive" move and then the options that follow: if the deception works what will happen and if the deceptive move doesn't work what will happen? All in the blink of an eye!

I grew up with old practice plans – there were no places for coaches to research, so they did what THEY were taught. There was no internet for my coaches in the '80's. But for some reason, these old drills still form a considerable part of the database for drills in TODAY's era. In essence, the drills have been updated to include visual practice plans, prewritten plans all with the intention of helping coaches. However, the focus needs to be on eliminating all plans where decision-making skills are not present. It is ok to do a flow drill for warmup purposes, to get loose and moving…after that – get into learning, and that means making decisions. (By the way, a 21st Century coach will do flow drills that incorporate decisions and endorse creativity.)

2. Use Reflective Thinking – to move forward

If we reject Isolation learning, recycled drills, over-emphasized strategy, and lack of skill building drills, how do we change?

In this section we have to look at ways we can improve the way we train youth hockey players:

A. Understand "Transfer of Training – how to take practice habits into our games
B. Understand Decision-making – and the significance of limited time
C. Replace Isolation and Script drills with game-like applications

A. Understand "Transfer of training"

The making of a "skilled play" – the key is transferring the newly learned skill INTO a hockey game!

The term "transfer of training" has emerged as perceptive coaches determined that there should always be a close relationship between practice and the real game. The closer the alignment – that is, the greater the similarities between a practice and a game – the more likely the players can successfully apply what they learn in practice to a game. HOW DO YOU ASSESS THE ALIGNMENT in your practice?

Purposeful practices and pertinent challenges, provide the framework for developing a vast range of enjoyable and realistic practice scenarios that simulate the demands of high-level competition while retaining the crucial element of the play.

What is tactically desirable must be technically possible – but at what completion rate? Many coaches expect too much regarding the desired outcome. If coaches could learn that cognitive recognition is being built with every blunder, mistake or misread, then we could overcome the high expectation for perfect practice and instead celebrate the opportunity to make quick decisions and have five teammates react to a positive AND negative outcome. Both are necessary to be successful.

Coaches must emphasize the importance of efficiency, which is simply more player learning per minute and less players watching per minute. Coaches must emphasize maximum player participation. Coaches must emphasize maximum alignment between a practice and a game. Alignment / perfect practice - both mean the same thing – which is to learn a skill under the conditions as similar as possible to the environment in which the new learning will be applied. I.e. A game!!!

Coaches must provide the framework for realistic practice scenarios that can simulate the demands of high-level competition while retaining the crucial element of "game."

It is important here to highlight what I mean by high-level competition. Let's take the example of a Bantam team and the application of a defenseman to use a "REVERSE." (A reverse is when a defenseman collects a puck that has been dumped into his defensive zone and after collecting the puck skates around the back of his own net. His partner defenseman will yell out "reverse" whereby the puck carrying defenseman will bounce the puck off the end boards in the opposite direction he is skating and his partner can collect this pass.) By Bantam most defenseman should understand this particular play and my bet is that in a game against a weak opponent this play will be easy to execute. BUT, good coaches must recognize the challenge of identifying the proper time to execute this play against a team that is BETTER than you. Challenging your team to make plays at high-level must be extremely difficult and puts players at the edge of their abilities to read and react.

Every thirsty hockey player loves the process of practicing and learning under realistic, competitive scenarios.

B. Understand decision-making and the significance of limited time

An understanding of tactics is the glue that binds a team together. Remember, tactics is a series of skilled plays strung together. When every player understands and applies vital tactics, the team then becomes more than the sum of its individual parts. This is undoubtedly true. By focusing on tactical plays increases the ability of all players to see the same problems and possibilities at the same time resulting in an almost telepathic understanding. This builds trust, and it can lead to that powerful yet intangible motivational force – team spirit.

To allow for more tactical hockey development, coaches can reduce the time they typically spend on teaching SYSTEMS and spend more time on stringing skillful plays together. The surefire way to spend less time on STRATEGY is to keep the STRATEGY simple! By keeping the strategy simplified enables a coach to place more emphasis on "skill building" which will always benefit players more in the long term. It may result in less wins but it will definitely result in more players going on to Junior or College.

Stringing together multiple skill plays hones a player's GAME SENSE. The ugliest thing I hear is -> many coaches do not believe that GAME SENSE can be improved. This belief is a complete cop out. What a coach is really saying by believing that GAME SENSE can't be improved is this: "I don't know how to enhance the game sense of most of my players."

This coach hides behind the statement that it can't be done. What baloney. Game sense can be improved. Some players get it very quickly and others take much longer, but constant attention must be made to the environment in which this skill can be improved. The environment must be pressurized. Pressurized to react quickly and with limited time. Pressurized because of opposing players trying their best to outwit each of your decisions.

There must be a continual interaction among technique, tactics, and strategy in hockey.

Players with "Game sense" have the ability to:

      I.   READ and INTERPRET their views;

     II.   Make APPROPRIATE decisions; and

    III.   EXECUTE those decisions

ALL IN A SPLIT SECOND!

Skilled play is often referred to as Hockey Sense which is bridging the gap between understanding and action and incorporating the process of decision making, which is a critical aspect of a game.

So, why do we dump the puck out, or dump it in, or shoot it away from our goalie? Enhancing game sense will help players to better interpret their own experience and draw wisdom from their past experiences to add critical thinking – what else COULD I DO?

C. Replace Isolation and Script drills with game-like applications

In a youth hockey game a player might maintain possession of the puck for under 20 seconds and for the remainder of the game, the player must skillfully play without the puck. Continually adjusting, supporting, gathering information, making decisions on whether to pressure, to defend, to pinch, to intercept, to find time, to anticipate teammates reaction to a scenario, to purposefully find open space are just a few skills away from the puck. And in my opinion, we spend far too much time practicing without scenarios that allow young players to improve the above skills.

The problem in hockey is that while new data is pouring in, players are trying to execute decisions with data coming at them from all directions and at different speeds. To be a great hockey player, you must learn how to be a grandmaster chess player in a chess game that features "pieces that are constantly moving." (Imagine a grandmaster chess player considering his next move and BAM the board just changed, and BAM it changed again...seems to me, chess is easier!)

For example: A player could rapidly accelerate into position to gain possession of the puck, control the puck or instantly redirect the puck all the while dealing with a powerful physical challenge from the opponent. This overlap of accurate data retrieval and acquisition, rapid interpretation and prediction, clear decision making, and physical execution, are all carried out in milliseconds, often while fatigued or emotionally stretched, is what makes the great hockey players great.

So, while the notion that the player reads the view, interprets it, decides what to do, and then reacts may represent an acceptable theoretical model, its simplistic nature has SIGNIFICANT LIMITATIONS in helping to understand the nature of skilled performance in hockey because:

- The view is not static, in fact, the sequence of action is complex and continually changing;
- The interpretation is based on the assumption that your teammate will react according to your decision; and
- The action is tied to TIME, the amount of time this skill play will take is a critical factor in making a skilled play.

Time becomes important. Where opponents focus on limiting time, players face challenges:

- Players must interpret mass information with little or no information from a static image; rather players must make multiple assumptions in deciding what the best option may be all the while possessing the technique to complete the task under extreme duress.
- The ability to read the view while players are about to control the puck means that they can decide what they are going to do even before the puck arrives. This is an

important OVERLAP of the phases. Compressing time between reading the play and executing the desired action is critical to developing hockey sense. Observation and taking action must overlap. Players will become intuitive (instantly access past experience to solve problems).

Skilled players learn to "save" time, no matter how small which enables players to execute a perfect play which may only become obvious because of the player's ability to "save" time. Deception is the art-form of saving time and is used by great players on almost every shift. Skilled players seem to have all the time in the world because they have "chunked" perceptive information into MEANINGFUL PATTERNS which allow players to "speed up the process" and make better decisions. The process of drawing together all of the required elements to instantly solve a problem as posed by the opposition or even a teammate.

3. Begin the Paradigm Shift - Innovation

Practice: Can we create challenging and enjoyable practice situations through which players young and old can be motivated to play their way to understanding, competence and excellence?

By using carefully structured plans to achieve specific outcomes coaches must throw away conventional practice plans that do not meet the requirements of game-situation learning. Toss out the: you go here, pass puck there, skate over here, get pass back...it is just one big "script" and hinders development.

A coach can innovate by simply adopting the following into their plans:

 A. Effective use of small area games
 B. 21st Century Enjoyment
 C. Things to consider when adopting small area games
 D. Enhance small area game competition
 E. Excellent - Practice Expectations

A. Effective use of Small Area Games

Small-area games are game-like competitive drills that utilize a playing surface that has been reduced in size. A typical small-area game will be played in one end of the ice and can be played cross-ice, between face-off dots, in one corner, below the faceoff dots or in any other number of areas, including the neutral zone.

Small-area games are created to mimic different situations that are seen in a regular game. While games can be played without any special rules or conditions, it is usually these small rule modifications that keep the games fresh and allow players to see many different offensive and defensive situations.

Small-area games are designed to focus on multiple skills and situations, increasing puck touches and situational repetition. During a small-area game, players will have more puck touches because of the reduced size of the playing area, the reduced number of players and the special conditions placed on each game.

Small area games limit decision-making TIME. This is a vital piece of why playing these games are so important. Time had been reduced, therefore, decision-making skills will be enhanced. Players are constantly put into situations of duress and can only solve these situations with quick skill making and decision making plays. "Thinking" skills are developed. Failure is constant. Success is surprising. If you learn to play in limited time, these scales will eventually be flipped from failure ever present to success becoming constant. Then the game changes and the process repeats itself. Taking time away from players is absolutely the best way possible to develop hockey sense. Players can become intuitive (instantly access past experience to solve problems) SECOND time I wrote this!

An often overlooked benefit of small-area games is the positive effect they have on goaltenders. Goaltenders, arguably the most important part of any team, are often the most neglected players in practice. Most drills provide shots that either don't challenge the goaltenders, come so quickly that the goaltender does not have time to recover properly, or come at a pace that does not adequately duplicate conditions seen in a real game. Goaltenders thrive in small-area games because they are seeing live competition and much like a skater getting quality puck touches goalies can face as many shots in one ten minute small-area game as they will possibly see in an entire regulation game.

Small-area games produce situations that our players will see time and again in game speed competition. Through trial and error, they will develop many different options to create plays and experience success.

Small-area games create a more competitive practice environment. Competition is fun. More than that, small-area games push players to work harder, compete at game speed and learn to succeed against the competition.

Small-area games provide an intense environment in which to train while maintaining a proper work-to-rest ratio for players. Coaches using small-area games in place of traditional conditioning drills will find that their players are more willing to work hard in practice because they are having fun and competing. Players will almost always ask for one more shift in a small-area game.

Small-area games keep more players moving! With less resting!

Small-area games develop and improve individual and team skills. Chunking skills are enhanced because players can see patterns more often allowing players to identify earlier the tactical combinations that are needed to solve offensive and defensive advantages. Players can develop and improve every skill related to the game of hockey through the use of small area games.

Players learn to excel in tight situations. The modern game of hockey is played in small areas and in tight situations. As players continue to get bigger, stronger and faster, the rink continues to shrink and there is less room to execute. Training to play in these situations through the use of small-area games will strengthen players and teams by practicing for these tight playing conditions on a daily basis. As players get more comfortable playing and practicing in small areas, they are better able to execute skills and systems in competition. Your players will develop game strategies, make better decisions and have greater enthusiasm for practice. The bottom line is, when players see a situation develop in a game that they have seen hundreds of times before, the will know how to handle it. Players can't be expected to make proper decisions and go to the right place on the ice during a game if they have never been trained to do it in practice!

Where does hockey sense come from? For some players it may be an inborn trait, but for most players hockey sense comes through experience. If they're not on the outdoor rinks playing pick-up hockey, where is that experience going to come from? It has to be built into practices. Virtually any individual or team skill can be taught through the use of small-area games.

This is accomplished in a learning-friendly environment in which the players are having fun. As a coach, have the courage to allow players to figure things out for themselves and let the game teach the game. Here is a very brief look at some of the skills commonly taught through the use of small-area games:

Skating. Every skating maneuver is needed in small-area games. Lateral movement, stops and starts, tight turns, transitions, crossovers and the forward and backward stride will all be practiced in virtually every game.

Passing. Nearly every game incorporates passing as an integral part of the game. Rules can be applied to games requiring a number of passes prior to a shot on net or require players to give and receive passes from support players.

Shooting. No traditional drill will allow players to attempt as many shots under competitive playing conditions as a typical small-area game. Players are encouraged and required to use a variety of different shots, including the nearly-ignored backhand, and attack the net to capitalize on rebounds.

Stickhandling. Every player has the opportunity to handle the puck a great deal in small-area games. More than simply handling the puck, they're required to do it in tight areas and under pressure. In my experience, this is the optimal way to become a better puckhandler.

Transitioning. One of the trademarks of small-area games are the continual transitions players must make from offense to defense. Forwards and defensemen alike are put into situations that they would rarely, if ever, see in a traditional drill; yet routinely have to face during actual competition.

Angling. Because defenders are placed into a variety of real-game situations in small areas, they learn to close gaps and cut angles with a great deal of skill.

Breakouts. Games can be designed to incorporate breakouts and forechecks. This creates an excellent opportunity for teams to practice specific plays during a live, competitive situation.

Power plays. Many small-area games provide odd-man situations that closely replicate typical power play alignments such as the overload and the umbrella. Conditions and rules regarding the number of players on each team and their positioning can be implemented to meet specific needs.

Puck support. To achieve success in most any small-area game, players must learn to properly support the puck carrier and position themselves to receive passes, anticipate turnovers and run interference for teammates.

Hockey sense. Hockey sense is a skill that many coaches do not teach. The coach needs only to shape the situations that the players learn to enhance hockey sense. Players will gain hockey sense through experience and repetition during game-like pressurized situations. Over the course of a season, small-area games can give players hundreds of quality game-like repetitions in various situations that are commonly seen in real their league games. Traditional drills are all too often scripted, eliminating the thought process and decision making skills. Outcomes of small-area games, while containing specific guidelines and rules, are never predetermined.

B. 21st Century Enjoyment

One of the most critical pieces for youth hockey players is to LIKE coming to practice. Moreover, I can assure you that when practices are full of competitions and game-like situations, you really feel the intensity heat up as the skills are constantly being fired and misfired.

The real attraction of hockey is the pleasure that players experience when a movement task is done well; the sweet feeling of making a crisp pass or shooting the puck exactly where you wanted to; the satisfaction of an intelligent play that produces a scoring chance or the thoughtful interception of a defender reading the offensive play; the enjoyment gained from a growing sense of improvement and mastery of skills learned and transferred from a practice to a game.

I can guarantee that small area games include the most important element of youth hockey – they are fun to play.

C. Things to consider when adopting small area games:

Motivate

What are the powerful forces behind students with the motivation to pursue excellence? Learners must make a commitment to mastery, the amount of time players spend practicing, and the degree of alignment of that practice. These are irrelevant without the desire to succeed.

"The most exceptional performers in hockey are driven by an obsessive desire to succeed. The ability to manage success and to deal with failure, without allowing either of these imposters to affect their performance is critical to achieving true potential." Quote

Using small area games to motivate competition between teammates is a surefire way to learn more quickly. Players don't like to lose, so anything a coach can do to motivate players to compete is a win-win scenario.

Failure

It is ok for a player to learn cognitively through a process where a player does not have enough time to complete the desired outcome, and as a result, the situation has changed, and new information must be collected. If coaches could promote the idea that mistakes and failure are a small price to pay for such experiences, and that the challenge of reading the display and reacting in a way that the coach wants is an excellent way to achieve overall success. Persistence. Resilience. Challenge.

Shaping Practice

Coaches must SHAPE a practice by thinking about intended outcomes and teaching points. Both intended teaching points and unintended teaching points can be utilized to steer player development. Coaches should put parameters on each small area game to get the intended teaching point to show up more often. Steer the outcome of the situation – try making it favorable to one side or try scoring points for a desired play instead of a goal.

Small area games allow for fewer players per game which equals more opportunities to learn, to perfect technique, to improve decision making. And less time to rest!

Attacker to Defender ratio:

Many times in hockey in order to develop the "correct" decision making skill, it becomes necessary to reduce the opponents until the desired outcome is achieved. However, minimizing the opponent to ZERO will, in fact, reduce a player's ability to make quick decisions. At the elite level, hockey players can be challenged to make quick decisions with an outnumbered defender to attacker ratio. Could a skillful team breakout 5 vs. 6?

Playing area

Who needs more space – beginners or elite performers? The answer is beginners. They will learn more quickly with more space with which to deal with getting good "displays" of the game, but elite players must learn to play in limited space. There is very little upside to practicing your team using the full ice. Instead, scenarios should be addressed where turnovers are caused and decisions made to convert opponent's mistakes turns into a feeding frenzy of scoring chances.

Freeze – stop where you are!

Freeze must seldom be intervened because of players' dislike of frequent disruption. We have all used this tactic to recreate the last teaching moment that we "can't let go." This tactic is excruciating for players. Rolling eyes and useless attention causes the "freeze where you are" to be fruitless. Use this tactic rarely.

Freeze replay helps to deliver a key concept by a coach's ability to restate the technical improvements needed for a particular play. And I have never seen a coach blow the whistle – recreate a play and say "well done, that is exactly what I wanted." Instead coaches look for a moment of negative action and can't stop themselves from using the scenario to "teach the team" by drawing out the negative points and pushing the "proper way" onto the situation.

Consider allowing teams to call tactical 30-second player only meetings to discuss what they are doing and how they might collectively work better together and incorporate the teaching point into the drill. This gets their accountability to rise and they can take ownership of tactically working together on stringing skillful plays in a row.

D. Enhance – small area game competition

Perfect practice enhances the maximum enjoyment and improvement of EVERY player. Players improve most rapidly when they are absolutely committed to mastering the task. This means that coaches can employ a variety of motivational strategies to induce player competition and engagement. Consider a roll over for the losing team or a jumping jack; these simple acts quickly remind players that there is a competition and most players want to win no matter the ridiculous punishment.

USA hockey loves the game of x and o's onto the ice. Imagine a small area game of 3 v 3 at one end of the rink. A coach diagrams a hashtag with a marker right onto the ice playing surface. When one team scores a goal (or performs the particular task at hand) a player from the scoring team races over to the game, drops his glove, picks up the marker and draws his or her team's X into an open area. The team will spend precious seconds defending short-handedly while their teammate thinks about where to place the X. Early in the game, this decision is easy. This continues until the tic-tac-toe game has either 3 X's or 3 O's in a row, just like the real game. The hilarious part of this game is that the same player is not allowed to put an X on the hashtag until each of his teammates has put an X on the hashtag. This creates confusion each time a player comes to the X and O board on the ice because they haven't seen the game progress. Many hasty decisions lead to losing the X and O game. It is a great game to watch decision-making skills.

E. Excellent - Practice Expectations

The coach's personality and skill are important factors. Those who are liked, admired, or simply respected by their team will always draw greater commitment and improved individual performance. Great coaches have high expectations for themselves and their team, and they insist that everyone strive to meet the team and individual expectations. If this can be done, the scene is set for remarkable things to happen.

The commitment level from the most reluctant players will be enhanced, and players and assistant coaches can benefit from knowing exactly what is expected of them at practice:

Players understand exactly what is expected of them in each learning piece of the practice
- Players see the task as worthwhile and achievable
- Players can see their learning improves their repetitions
- Players understand the application of the drill into a game situation
- Practices have game-like speed
- Players make choices and solve problems – sometimes successfully and sometimes unsuccessfully
- Players use repetition to improve a technique combined with a forced decision
- Coaches can monitor and record challenges to see improvement
- Practices are fashioned like building blocks, one drill MUST feed into the next drill and must be noticeable so that the "building" is understood by the players

Note: a great coach includes himself or herself for blaming team performance. Imagine a team has an abysmal performance – weak effort, dismal execution or whatever may have contributed to the poor performance. Instead of thinking about "skating the team" consider this: "skate with the team" for you are part of the team. Did you have your BEST performance while the team struggled? I doubt it. So either get over it or try to figure out what went wrong, but before you lay blame on your team, know that you are part OF IT.

"And I think, as a player, I'm always trying to find ways to get better and challenge myself, get myself into areas where it doesn't feel comfortable."

- John Tavares

Chapter 2

What MAKES McDavid and Matthews so GOOD?

They both grew up with premium, innovative skills coaches! And an insatiable appetite to WANT to learn.

Ronals Sullivan revealed this story to us in 1975: A visiting coach asked Anatoly Tarasov in 1974 to reveal his Russian coaching secrets. "Do you think we have secrets?" Tarasov replied. "Today's secret is tomorrow's common knowledge. All you have to do is look. There is no secret in hockey. There is imagination, hard work, discipline and dedication to achieving whatever the goal is. But there are no secrets, none at all."

Tarasov believed that a hockey player "must have the wisdom of a chess player, the accuracy of a sniper and the rhythm of a musician." But more important, he said, "He must be a superb athlete." Anatoly Tarasov, 76 at the time of his death, was one of hockey's most innovative coaches and saw the game like a conductor sees his band.

The story of secrets continues to loom today as if there are freaks of nature that just simply posess better skills than the rest of us. I am here today to tell you that the secret is out of the bag, and those pundits that believe in freak athleticism are WRONG!

There are tons of people out there who are always looking for the easy way. For most, this is the norm. As a society, we see the wealthiest and admire the fastest, but we tend to see these types of people as outliers. The wealthiest must have been handed a gift to them, the gift of intelligence, the gift of access to capital, the gift of better schooling, and the list goes on for reasons why it can't be me.

The same goes for sport. Why are some athletes so great? They must have a god-given talent given to them. The anwser is – you are right! They do have a gift – and the gift is -> the OBSESSION to get better. And the athletes that obsess and combine it with professional help can really poke above the clouds into stratespheric capabilities.

Let's have a look at Marshall Faulk, a running back in the NFL. Well, actually a hall of fame running back. The perception is that Marshall Faulk is a natural. Freaky ability to read plays. Freaky ability to scamper one step ahead of all of the defenders. What do you think? Marshall Faulk was both a running back and receiver for the St. Louis Rams. In 2002, Faulk had just become the first player to gain a combined two thousand rushing and receiving yards in four consecutive seasons.

Faulk's uncanny skill at knowing where every player is on the football field at all times is freaky. Somehow, he cannot only see the defense prior to the snap, but also predict and correctly read their behaviour in the milliesecond DURING a play. In all that chaos of an NFL play, Faulk knows what the defense is trying to do, where they are on the field, and he can feel what is ABOUT to happen...

According to his teammates, he's never wrong. Insane. But is it insane how he can read the plays? Faulk doesn't think so. He explains that he spent years and years watching football. And after every play he always considered the question: Why? In high school he sold hot dogs at the New Orleans Superdome stadium for the sole purpose of studying the game (you can probably sell a lot of hot dogs and never miss a play in football!). His main mission was to "figure out" what was going on and "why" plays work the way they do.

"That question basically got me involved in football in a more in-depth way," said Faulk, "I just wanted to know: 'Well, why are we running this play? Why are we attacking it this way? Why are they doing that? Why are they doing this?' Before you know it, you're learning more, and before you know it, the easier it is to do your job." As a pro, he never stopped asking why and probing deeper into the workings of the game.

If you stop and ask yourself, "how did Marshall Faulk have such an incredbile ability to read and react to plays?" The answer is that Faulk prepared himself to see the plays. Was it a "natural talent?" Did he possess the highest football IQ of any football player? Or did he study the game like a grandmaster studies chess?

"The point, rather, is that although talent feels and looks predestined, in fact we have a good deal of control over what skills we develop, and we each have more potential than we might ever presume to guess," explains Daniel Coyle in the Talent Code.

Of course, there are many factors that come into play when trying to get to the bottom of What Makes Connor McDavid and Auston Matthews so good. I am going to go out on a limb here and tell you that they both match Marshall Faulk's insatiable thirst to learn more. And it is only natural to presume that you can learn WAY more with a grand master coach at your side. Auston Matthews and Connor McDavid both received superior training at a very young age in combination with their growing obsession to be the best. These two players were taught NHL level skills from a very early age.

Darryl Belfry, the current skills coach for Auston Matthews, explains, "As a player, the most debilitating habits are the ones that lead you to success at your current level, but become irrelevant as you move up, level to level. Relying on a set of skills that are irrelevant is among the top issues that prevent players to project to higher performance levels of hockey."

Each player was able to commit the time to master high end, NHL caliber skills. Time. Money. Repeat. I am also 100% confident that their skills coaches are not boasting that each player that spends time and money with them will get them a direct pass to play in the NHL – it does not work that way. I can, however, assure you that players with the right drive, focus, a determination will benefit HUGELY from training with high-end skills coaches. By hugely, here is what I mean – if you begin as a good athlete, and excel at any sport you touch, you will likely improve to the point of -> college level hockey player, which is the goal of many players and parents (realistic? Hmmm..."more" realistic is a better choice of words. That is of course if your determination is tied directly to obsession, a burning desire to succeed.)

Connor McDavid (CM) practiced his on-ice skills in a way that few others did. He was able to get the most out of a high-end skating/skills coach from a very young age. His attention to detail was unparalleled. CM and his skating coach agreed on the unorthodox principle – focus on acceleration at all times. When the rest of us (average NHLers) want to slow down (enabling us to benefit from more time and space), CM's modus operendi was to speed up. His principle shifted away from allowing *him* more time and space TO taking time and space away from his defenders. They can't defend me if I accelerate into them.

Connor McDavid and skills and skating coach Joe Quinn joined forces when Connor was just 9 years old. Here is what Quinn said about Connor's skill set, "With a lot of guys, if the feet are doing something, the hands aren't," Quinn said. "If the hands are trying to beat the opponent, the feet are in the glide position. They lose their speed and have to recreate energy. Connor doesn't have to do that because with the overloading he's had and his nervous system, he's a major, major multitasker."

This means that he can accelerate into opponents with his head up and puck handle without thinking.

The degree of difficulty goes through the roof when you ask a player to accelerate and combine it with making a "skilled play." Every sense in our bodies tells us that if we accelerate we won't be able to execute. This mindset is wrong only because most of us never practiced this way and were never comfortable in this execution. However, with CM, his focus was to continue to accelerate and fail and keep going at it until success began to show up. Success to CM is like throwing gasoline onto an already raging fire. CM had the obsession to master this skill, and the success was adding fuel to the fire.

Now let's say you like this concept, and as a parent, you think – how can I help my son/daughter? Where can I go to get this type of training?

Accelerate with the puck everywhere is innovation, and it is tied to a principle that has clarity. Accelerate into your defenders. Keep trying. Keep going. It will eventually get more comfortable for you. Success is just around the corner. The answer to the above question (where to get help) is a tough one – because many (most) coaches don't want this type of play coming from our forwards. Coaches shy away from turnovers.

CM got to practice this principle away from his team - with other players at the skills sessions, where his skills coach applauded the turnovers/mistakes and injected feedback to enable future success.

It is almost impossible for a head coach to spend the required time involved in teaching such a remarkable habit. However, that does not mean it should be ignored either. The fundamental principle is -> accelerate any time you win a puck. Put the gas pedal to the floor.

Easy eh? Hmmm...there is a bit more to it.

We can all accelerate. The difficulty intertwined with this skill is to be able to do it with your head up. In fact, if you took out the accelerating principle and only focused on keeping your head up, your chances of going far in hockey just tripled.

Let's examine exactly what I mean. Think of any area on the ice and that you have just won a puck battle. Your first instinct needs to be COLLECT INFORMATION (Bob Gainey taught me that), and this relies on your ability to see clearly for up to 200 feet. Not 20 feet. Good players keep their necks and chins up, which allows for longer length vision; poorer players have an angle to their head that minimizes extensive vision. Try this right now -> look straight ahead, now, try angle and tilt your head, just minimally (like one inch) and notice the difference. It's huge. See for yourself.

Scenario: A defenseman out battles a forward in the corner of his defensive zone. Instinct #1 – get your head up. Combine Instinct #1 with #2 – which is to move your feet and accelerate out of this area. (Can you also add a deceptive move while accelerating? A fake? Use an eye fake or a skate fake to give false information all while using the first two instincts) Instinct #3 – Weigh your options for execution. These three instincts happen almost simultaneously. (Players that are able to throw a deceptive move into the mix, grab precious time to weigh options, time that is measured in tenths of a second, enjoy space to execute skill plays.)

A forward wins a puck in the offensive zone. The same exact progressions take place.

Now let's examine a puck that has ALREADY been won. For example, a defenseman heads towards his or her zone to retrieve a puck and has minimal pressure. Instinct #1 – head up. Instinct #2 – slow down, head to the back of the net. Instinct #3 – execute a set play. In this scenario, the defenseman is learning how NOT to make quick decisions -> instead, being coached to take the easy way out. I am not saying this is wrong, but I do think that if you play this way continuously, over time, your development is going to go backwards. Your decision-making skills become stunted, and you rely on set plays. I have always maintained that good hockey players show themselves the most at combine camps, or anything similar – where coaching is exceptionally minimal, and set-plays are out the window. (Imagine being a 17, 18-year-old rookie at a junior camp or a 19-year-old at an NHL camp – show your skills! Show them you can make fast and smart decisions. Don't look for the easy way out.)

Let's look at another example -> a center receives a good pass from his or her winger and enters the neutral zone with his or her head up. What are the center's thoughts? Option 1 – your offside winger should be getting in position to support you for a pass. Option 2 – avoid a turnover by dumping the puck into an area 'with purpose' for you and the winger. Option 3 – slow down and draw a defender in, using a chip ahead or find a late player in the NZ that has joined your attack. Option 4 – put the gas pedal down and beat the defense.

As a coach, you need to ask yourself -> what are my goals for this center? Are the center's own intentions to play a level higher than currently playing? To get the center to junior hockey? If these goals are matched with the coach – then the options listed above should be dwindling down to this: How can I (center) make a skilled play in this neutral zone? (Moreover, while having the confidence to try it.) How can I manipulate the defense to give my winger and I a chance to enter the zone? Can I use my vision to see behind the play and identify a late player that will become a useful option?

The job of a good coach is to put centers and defenseman into these situations 1000's of times, building up the "experience" bank. No scenario is the same, but many scenarios are incredibly similar. What worked before?

Auston Matthew's (AM) skill level is off the charts. He attributes most of the learning of the sick skills he has in his arsenal to the 100's of hours playing condensed area 3 on 3 as a youth hockey player. Hmmm...I played 1000's of hours of shinny hockey on outdoor rinks around Toronto. (Favorite ones were West Mall and Martingrove!) And I never learned the sick arsenal of skills AM did. Want to know why? Because he has sick skills coaches that helped him solve situation problems. Here is what teammate, Connor Carrick said about Matthews' skills, "I think he's just able to work at a little bit higher pace in those tighter situations. Some guys see traffic as something to avoid, something to slow down for. You almost see him look at numbers at the line and hit the gas, attack the line and bull-rush it."

AM played against older players and was forced to use advanced skills that were REPEATEDLY practiced with his skills coach. When you have an obsessed player, you can really turn the skill into a habit which is defined as -> knowing how and when to perform a skill, never once thinking about a play. It just "happened."

Joe Walsh, head coach of the San Francisco 49'ers talked about Joe Montana and how they would work on basic fundamentals that would bore a high school quarterback to death when Joe already had four super bowl rings. Joe understood the connection between the details involved in a "basic" skill and to play as long as he could. His mastery of these details were what sustained his success. "You never stop learning, perfecting, refining – molding your skills." Joe Walsh.

AM doesn't "think" when he uses his silky puck handling skills, a set of skills that have been ingrained in his repertoire of habits. Instead, he used hard work. Here is what his skills coach had to say, "People will say, 'Wow, this kid is coming from Arizona – this is just a miracle,'" Boris Dorozhenko said. "But he was an absolutely normal kid. Athletic. Co-ordinated. He always had a little bit better hands and could surprise everybody with a little bit of puckhandling. But every year his talent was increasing by hard work. He put in very hard work to increase his talent."

Boris further explains, "Repetition is the key to success. It allows the player to focus not on skating, stick handling, or shooting. It frees the player's mind, allowing him to focus on individual creativity that is now the heart of the game."

Make Hockey Great Again

When AM went to the NTDP (National Training Development Program for the USA's best high schoolers, grades 11 and 12) as one of the best 15-year-olds in the country, Don Granato couldn't believe AM's skillful hands, but Don also couldn't believe that this kid had no idea how to actually PLAY hockey.

Don took him anyway, knowing that deep down he could teach this player "how" to play the game. He knew that it is much easier to teach AM how to play than it is to teach him how to puck handle with incredible poise. Don also felt with a program like the NTDP; AM could become a serious threat to become a future superstar. Don was right. Don is a superstar, and every coach should follow him.

Don also knew how to coach a group of the country's top 15/16-year-old players. He knew that most of these players possessed incredible skills, yet many of them didn't know how to use "other" players on the ice. The ability to play using each other is a critical piece for playing hockey at the higher levels – NCAA, CHL and the NHL. Don is an expert at letting these players play in game situations and letting the players solve problems on their own. Don sets up games and he adds in a set of rules and consequences, which brings out the competitiveness in every practice. Don is an inspiration to this book. Everybody should be adopting his principles.

Don knows the role of deliberate practice, the acquisition of skill needed for expert performance. He knows it takes time. But Don is the master of efficiency and realizes that his 80 minutes on the ice each day form a HUGE benefit to his players. Don doesn't waste a single minute.

Skill Progress

All hockey players progress. We all progress at different rates. The constant question is: how can I increase the pace of learning and mastering skills? Isn't that what we all want? Faster.

Let's take a look at the 4 basic skills: skating, puckhandling, shooting and passing.

These are the basics, like writing these sentences to string this book together in a meaningful way. But man, these basics are tough. And I want to point out to everyone that all the basic skills listed above are not basic – they are COMPLEX skills. In fact, they are so complex that most hockey coaches don't dare give feedback to these basic skills. The reason is that most coaches don't know how to improve these four "basic" skills.

How do I make my Peewee team better skaters? How do I make my WHL or USHL team better at skating? The same question comes into play at either level.

Shooting a puck is very similar to swinging a golf club. Have you ever taken a golf lesson and walked away with the feeling that the "new and improved" way to swing the club feels terrible? And the likelihood of staying with the new and improved way fades very quickly unless you sign up for another lesson.

The basics are really never taught in hockey. We put kids in their skates and let them loose! And 5 years later, some kids became efficient and other kids continue to struggle, but there really is no instruction for young kids learning to skate effectively. The same goes for shooting, passing and puckhandling.

Hmmm, last time I saw a AAA hockey coach teaching these "basic" skills...ahh never. So, if your coach isn't teaching you how to improve these skills, then who is?

The point I want to make in this section of Skill Progress is that our young players need constant attention on improving their technique. Puckhandling and Shooting don't even need ice for improvement! Skating needs ice. Passing is the one area where there are no specialized coaches – yet! But passing could be seen as the MOST important piece of a hockey team's skill set.

Four ~~BASIC~~ COMPLEX Skills that need constant improvement

1. Skating

To be good at hockey for a really long time means that you have to be a great skater. Better than the rest of the players. And if you can skate better than everyone else, you will "love" hockey. And if you can't skate as well as your teammates, you will likely learn to dislike hockey.

When you are in the "learn to play" phase, the most critical component to becoming a good player is - skating. As players become more proficient at this skill, it is vital to handle the puck while skating and performing skating exercises. Make no mistake, the best skaters will be the best hockey players for quite some time, quite possibly until they are 15-16 years old.

To become a great skater is relatively simple – you must skate many, many more miles than your competitors. A little instruction goes a long way too. I will list the most critical factors of a stride:

- Head up with tons of vision, even when doing drills without a puck;
- Knees bent deeply – this is very tough to do, as many kids do not have the strength to be engaged in a skating position for very long
- Torso upright – angle is unique to each skater, but we don't play hockey like speed skaters (bent over), and we don't play like figure skaters (completely upright).
- Full-length stride – to enable maximum push
- Body weight transfer from skate to skate
- Knees pushing out over toes of skate (deeply bent knees)
- Skates return to glide phase "straight" up the ice
- Violent return to glide phase with toe drive comes from an excellent heal kick

Now you are an expert on the forward stride! And now, we need to practice. There are many more technical pieces to skating – edges for stopping and turning, accelerating, decelerating, mini crossovers, backwards skating, pivoting, skulling, v-steps, Crosby's (10 and 2) just to mention a few. Mastering all these skating techniques will become critical to becoming a skilled hockey player.

MK on Skating Coaches

I see many youth hockey players taking skating lessons from figure skating coaches, and I am reluctant to agree that this is the best way to learn to skate more efficiently or enhance acceleration or stop and turn violently. Simply put, every single thing a figure skater does on the ice is pre-programmed. Rehearsed. That is why they call it a "figure skating routine." Hockey is the exact opposite. A hockey brain needs to learn to get as far away from rehearsal as possible.

I am, however, a fan of figure skaters edges. The way they can use deep edges and transition from edge to edge is an important part of great skating ability. The key should be to keep learning these edges in an environment that isn't always entirely structured to allow for the best possible outcome. The better way to train would be to figure out a way to have an unpredictable way to learn edges. Or at least progress to this point.

Balance and hockey go hand in hand together. So figure skaters that teach hockey players should be cognizant of the constant attack by opponents to put you OFF balance. Edges help, but so does body balance. Skating coaches must keep pushing against the player, pushing them off balance, working their core and keeping their deep knee position.

Ever bump into a SOLID person? A person that people just seem to bounce off, like walking into a coke machine? A wrestler comes to mind. An extremely low center of gravity, a core like an ox. This is how hockey players need to be when possessing and skating with the puck. And, I'm not sure figure skating coaches really understand this.

So if you had to look to get skating help, I would look at the speed skaters. Explosive starts. Massive attention to acceleration detail. Maximum push for acceleration. Driving the toes straight ahead. Efficient. Powerful. The speed skater knows how to accelerate straight ahead. They know how to push violently. They know how to train these muscles.

To be a great skater includes being able to accelerate and decelerate to a puck that is only 20 feet away. To be able to accelerate in an effort to get body position is far more critical than freewheeling up the ice. That time and space eventually dries up at the higher levels.

A mix between learning the deep edges from figure skaters and the violent acceleration of speed skaters would be ideal. Good luck finding them! I found Tony Meibock, USA Olympian in Calgary. In one summer, my overall speed from Tony teaching me how to skate efficiently went up massively. I went from being an above average skater to the top skater in the league, and this training propelled me all the way to the NHL.

Here is what Robert Mcleod wrote about McDavid in the Toronto Star, "*The Edmonton Oilers star stole the puck deep in the Anaheim end from Ducks defenseman Sami Vatanen, raced out toward the blueline to elude Vatanen, then suddenly reversed course at high speed and ripped a laser shot into the far top corner of the net. Boom. It was one of the top moments of the NHL postseason and left fans asking, "How did he do that?" It turns out, McDavid had practiced that exact move for years.*

"*It's a lot of edge work, doing everything fast,*" remarked McDavid about how he trains.

2. Puckhandling and Stickhandling (same thing)

Puckhandling is misunderstood in my opinion. This skill serves two purposes. The first is to actively move the puck back and forth in preparation for a deke, pass or shot. The second purpose is by far the most critical -> the action of moving the puck back and forth across the blade with skill and accompanied by ENABLING unbelievable vision. Great puck handlers never look down! Becoming a master at puck handling simply allows the player to take his/her focus away from the puck and onto the play. See, if you never need to look down, not even for what I call an 'eye flicker' which is basically a blink downwards, then you can use your entire vision to create hockey plays. Essentially the game slows down because you see everything with clarity.

> Evgeny Kuznetsov, Washington Capitals, Player's Tribune: "My father teach me, too. First thing, you never look at puck. Eyes always up. Look left, right, forward. You look down, it's over. Even now, if I look down at puck in a game, my dad let me know about it. He texts me."

The odd time you may see a skilled hockey player look down, but I know for sure that this move is used as deception in many instances. 'Faking' looking down can sometimes draw a defender to become vulnerable to want to step up and take a crack at throwing a body check, but a skilled forward will use this deceptive move (looking down) to create the vulnerability of the defenseman to want to hit, which usually leaves the defenseman looking for his jock. The look down move is also used to fool goaltenders into thinking that your options have floated away and that you are committed to shooting – deception again. These types of deceptive moves can only effectively be learned AFTER you become a master of puck handling.

The rhythm of the puck rolling between the forehand and backhand of the blade is the glue that allows a player never to have to look down. A skilled puck handler can feel the puck on the toe, middle or preferred heel of the stick. The unbelievable quickness of the hands, the centrifugal force of the back and forth frees up your brain to allow vision and the scenario before you to recall the best option available from previous experiences.

Ever notice how incredibly skilled players seem to have all the time in the world? Defenseman don't want to close the gap. The reason is that VISION is the scariest skill. The skilled player sees a defender closing in on him and has time to plan his escape, has tons of information to find a great play. No wonder defenseman don't want to attack skilled forwards with their head up.

> Tavares said. "And I think, as a player, I'm always trying to find ways to get better and challenge yourself, get yourself into areas where it doesn't feel comfortable. Indeed, with the stick handling and the puck work, combined with the edge work and creating space by moving your feet, that's certainly something I feel is significant."

To be an excellent puckhandler takes 1000's of hours of practice. But the great news is that it doesn't have to be done on the ice. There are thousands of videos of NHL'ers training off-ice.

Lastly, don't always go for the "hockey ball / Swedish hockey ball" which have weight to them and don't bounce much. In my opinion, using weighted balls is for beginners to learn because these balls don't bounce. To get really soft hands try handling a tennis ball with speed!

Skating and Puck Handling – Part II – keep 2 hands on the stick!

I think this is one of the easiest / hardest things to learn as a young hockey player. Too many coaches don't understand the importance of playing with two hands on the stick. If I had to name the areas on the ice where one hand is better than two, I could come up with ONLY one. – Backchecking. Everywhere else on the ice, two hands are preferable. I bet someone is thinking – what about a defenseman who is backing up and receiving the rush? Answer – that is old school defending. Or maybe, a forward is racing for a puck in the neutral zone for a breakaway – ok, I will give you that one. So two.

My favorite defenseman/offenseman to watch who plays the new, cutting-edge style is Drew Doughty. You can view Drew play 25+ minutes a game and dissect every one of his shifts, and you will notice that he lets go of his bottom hand for less than 20 seconds out of 25 minutes. I think that Drew is continuously thinking about 'how I can get the puck ON my stick,' and that isn't possible with one hand on his stick. Everywhere he goes – two hands.

The other thing that young hockey players can learn by using two hands is that you have to defend MORE with your feet and less with your reach. Every time you 'reach' to put your stick in the old-fashioned 'stick on puck' move that is still a widely accepted principle, the player becomes prone. And finding a defenseman in a prone position is precisely what a skilled forward is looking for. By using two hands, defenseman must learn to use their feet to put their body in good defending position, not their arms!

There will be times that using one hand can be more beneficial than two hands, but those times pale in comparison to the benefits of using two hands. A couple of examples of using one hand instead of two – getting your stick in the passing lane on the PK. When you are close to getting beat by a player skating wide on you, use one hand to take away the puck carrier's passing lanes. And that is about it.

Forwards also must learn to skate at full speed with two hands on the stick; to minimize the difference in top speed between the same player with one hand on the stick and two hands on the stick. This can be tricky. Most youth players are much faster with one hand on their stick (choo choo train elbows!). Close this gap and have the difference be minimal. Think of this – when you are attacking a defenseman using the CM principle, how many hands do you think you need to use to make a skillful offensive play? TWO! So it starts with practice.

The other great thing about having two hands on your stick is that it forces the player into a lower, more knee bent position. The actual position that allows players to move the best. To absorb hits the best. To be their strongest. Think about the faceoff. This square off involves the most fairly battled completion on the ice. One on one. Macho on Macho. Then think of the body position of these two centers? Look at how low they get. Their entire body position shrinks to 50% of its normal height. Get low, get balanced and get ready. You won't find more knee bend than when two centers faceoff. And of course they use two hands. Every puck battle including defending should have two hands. Period.

So when you begin your quest for higher level playing, remember that this skill is natural to accept, but must be strictly enforced by coaches of younger age groups. I often tell players and coaches that I can teach a player to take his bottom hand OFF the stick in about 1 minute, but it will take me a hundred hours to show him/her to keep it on the stick for long periods of time. Always err on the side of 2 hands ALL the time.

3. Releasing the puck, formerly known as shooting

Shooting has evolved, and the release is everything. The quickness of the puck leaving the blade is now known as – quick release.

There a few key principles to developing a great shot. The first principle is: power/velocity comes later. If a young player is worried about power, the quickness will never develop. The second principle is: the wind time must shrink cosiderably. This means that the time you decide you want to shoot the puck to the time the puck leaves the blade of your stick must be reduced. To generate power takes more time, therefore the more critical principle to learn for a youth hockey player is to release the puck quickly.

Youth hockey players spend way too much time practicing shooting the puck that are unilke shooting in game situations. Full power, blazing shots at the top corners of the net, ripping pucks off the glass! Instead, players should be focusing on shooting from areas on the ice where shots actually come from, and let me tell you, the middle of the slot is a once in 10 games shot. Youth players need to be encouraged to <u>move the puck before every shot.</u>

Here is the perfect world to learn to shoot: before every single shot that a youth hcokey player takes, a pair of shin pads pop up out of nowhere directly in front of the puck. How long would it take a player to learn to move the puck just before shooting? Pull it. Push it. Drag it. Let me tell you, those shin pads are coming as players get older.

The third principle to shooting the puck is: make your sweet spot as big as a fat tire. Players who can shoot the puck well from any position are deadly. It is tough to practice shooting pucks from in tight by your skates or using outstretched arms, but skills like this pay off. Big time.

Here is what Auston's dad Brian explained, "much of that unpredictable style can be credited to skills coach Darryl Belfry, who's worked with the younger Matthews It was mostly changing the angle, shooting off any foot, shooting in stride, adding elements of deception," the elder Matthews said of his son's focus during his sessions with Belfry. "It was hidden and disguised. Auston wanted no one to know when it was coming."

Matt Martin, a teammate of AM, explained, "He can really shoot from any angle in any position. I think it's deceptive. It's hard for goalies to know what he's going to do with the puck because he's such a good playmaker too that you can't just play his shot. He never really commits to just shooting. He leaves himself options, and when he does shoot it, it's pretty accurate."

The common element between teammate Martin and Matthew's father, Bob's, description is – deception/disguise.

For young players learning to shoot, it is extremely important to shed the 1970's (still taught today) wrist shot technique. Here it is: weight transfer, pull the puck back behind you and use the weight transfer to power the shot. Man is that old school. Yet I see it being taught every day.

Here is the new way to shoot: hands in the same position as puck handling, about one elbow separation on the shaft of the stick. The puck remains in the puck handling position in front of the body. Handle puck quickly back and forth and fire the top hand out away from your chest – then with as much force as possible, pull back hard on the top hand toward your chest while pressing forward on the bottom hand, turning the stick into an elastic band and creating at least 10cm of flex in the stick. Flexing the stick comes partly from shifting your weight to the strongside skate (skate closest to the puck). Strongside knee bent, knee ahead of toes of skates. The other part of the flex comes from pulling and pushing the stick.

I ask youth hockey players and coaches all the time if Phil Kessel uses a 75 flex, what flex do you use? The answer: You guessed it, most players Bantam (barely 100lbs) aged and up are using 75 or more, and I can guarantee that 99% of these players are not as strong as perennial 40 goal scorer, Phil. Why does the average Bantam player feel that they should be using a flex similar to that of Kessel? There seems to be a weird, macho race to go up in stick flex. But the real macho player on every team is the player that can consistently get 10cm of flex on every wrist shot.

For younger players, have a look at your stick carefully and don't try to go up so fast in flex and circumference of your stick. At least two fingers need to wrap the entire stick and touch your palm on the other side when holding the stick in the store. The stick needs to bend super EASILY in the store. It is a lot tougher to flex a stick while skating than it is in your shoes putting your body weight onto the stick.

4. Passing - A lot has changed here too!

If you are like me, we agree that passing can be the most critical component to the game of hockey. Before I get into this section, I want to tell you two great personal stories about passing.

I was lucky enough to play 13 games for the Toronto Maple Leafs. I never even dreamed of this because I was a realist. Anyway, after I retired I signed up for the Alumni. One piece of this amazing organization is that the Alumni play various charity games around the city and country raising money for good causes. Games are usually played against local Police/Fire departments, insurance groups, you name it. With 13 games comes relative obscurity, so I was happy to be called to a few games when the player count got low.

I walk into an arena in Mississauga and find my way to the Leafs Alumni dressing room, and the first thing I see hanging up in the room – the #27 sweater. I actually got goose bumps knowing that Darryl Sittler was going to be playing in this game. Awesome. He was a hero for me growing up.

Lou Franceschetti announces 1 minute before we go out for warmup, the lines for the game, to which I only remember this: McLlwain, Sittler, Kennedy. What? Did he just say I am playing with Sittler? Holy cow. I am so glad I invited a bunch of my pals to come to the game. They wouldn't believe me if they didn't come. Then Lou makes a beeline toward me and sternly looks me straight in the eye – "number 27 shoots" and then he jumps on the ice and warmup begins. What? What did he just say? What the heck does that mean? So I am skating around the ice and my thoughts are still – I can't believe I read the children's book about when Daryl scores 10 points in a single game (still an NHL record) to my son, Owen, about a 1000 times. Seconds later I pop out of my daydream and I pass a puck to Darryl who is smoothly skating towards the slot, he accepts the pass and he shoots into the empty net. And then it hits me, I figured out what Lou meant – <u>YOU DON'T</u> SHOOT! (You pass to #27 all night long.) Ok, no problem, I got this.

Daryl got two goals, I got two assists (no shots on net!) and my favorite part of the whole experience was when I made my best pass to Darryl and he had a perfect chance for the hat-trick. All alone in the slot, he missed wide and then slapped his stick on the ice as if that was the only one he missed in his whole life. He told me after that that was his last game for the Alumni – not sure if it was or not, but that was a really cool moment for me, perhaps I assisted on his last two goals. That's what I say anyway.

The second story comes from a small town north-west of Toronto, called Tottenham. My sister and I lived with our Mom in Tottenham for three years. Basically from grades 3-5. The town was a "C" town based on population size and our team was good enough to play the "B" sized towns. At the end of the season, the players and parents filled the local town rink and trophies and awards were handed out. There was only ONE individual award presented and it went to the player from any age group who compiled the most assists over the course of the season. That player would have their name painted in the rink. I looked at my mom and said, "I'm getting that next year." She looked at me and smiled and probably thought to herself - the carrot has been dangled, he is obsessed. You guessed it - my name is painted in that rink!

Back to the book. Passing is the most rewarding part of the game. Passing is the beauty of the game. Tic, tac, toe. Give and go. Telepathic senses. Knowing where players are going to be and putting the puck right on their tape...satisfaction.

This important element is, however, yielded at the lower age groups. Not enough emphasis is placed on developing this skill. Skating yes. Shooting yes. Puck control yes. But passing is so difficult that many coaches wait until player's abilities improve before focusing on this crucial skill. A coach that knows hockey also knows the effect that precision passing has on any game.

It is extremely important to structure passing skills to be within a random environment. Once again, if the coach diagrams up a passing play that has no decision-making, the drill loses its skill-building effect. Passing from one stationary player to another is a good introductory way for kids that are just learning. After that though, for passing to be mastered, all passing activities must involve BOTH players skating. When one player is passing from a stationary position, the passer's skills hardly develop at all. I often use this expression -> my grandmother can't skate, but I could put her in this drill and she could swat pucks to players. Useless.

But when diagramming up a drill that involves BOTH players skating, the drill becomes infinitely tougher. I recently coached a High School team that struggled making passes to each other skating around the rink in partners! The point is – passing is a tough, long and sometimes painful road but it must be developed the whole way through.

TIP: Coaches need to listen to higher level players passing the puck around. Listen to a JR. or NHL warmup or practice. This is what you will hear: a tree branch breaking, snap. Snap. Every time a player receives a pass – snap.

There are two reasons for this. 1. We pass the puck way harder than we used to. 2. The stick blades are stiff and accept these bullet passes with ease.

The key: to catch a hard pass a player must catch the puck on the back half of the blade of their stick - the heel side. Any pass that is caught from the middle to the toe will explode off of your stick.

The 1980's way that I got taught to catch a pass: "cradle the puck and catch it like an egg, no sound, a gentle sweep backwards as the puck arrives on your stick." Holy cow, that technique is so old it's in black and white.

MK Thoughts - Another good coach - YouTube

Wow what a resource we have as coaches and players. We can look at clips over and over. Players that really want to master becoming better hockey players can watch hockey plays to develop "hockey sense." Same thing as Marshall Faulk. Watch. Watch more closely. Ask why. And then practice.

More young players need to watch and learn. Not just watch, try to figure out what is happening and how players are solving problems.

Evegny Kuznetsov, explains, "How much do I love hockey? I can't even describe. In Russia, we don't really have a Christmas break, but from December 31 to January 3, everything closed. Even hockey school. These were the worst days of my life. Four days with no hockey, I get so depressed. I can't even sleep. Just sit watching YouTube of Kovalev and wait. I didn't have a computer at home. My friend got one, so we would all sit there for two hours watching YouTube, seeing how guys are playing."

As soon as the break was over, "Then we go onto the ice and try to do the same things."

Advanced skill building

There are 4 basic skills that Auston Matthews and Connor McDavid got a ton of help with as they progressed through their youth hockey levels. But, there seems to be an endless break down and analysis of the game that keeps players improving.

I heard recently that skill building is over by the time you reach 16 years old. That may be partly true. I definitely think you can improve many more areas including: recognition skills and learning to manipulate players to gain advantages.

I am a big fan of Glenn Carnegie and I wanted to introduce a skill that I had never really thought about, but the way Glenn outlines the skills makes me wish I had the pleasure of learning from him when I was a pro.

Glenn Carnegie, skills coach for the Vancouver Canucks. Glenn talks at a conference about how he works with Bo Horvat. The particular skill that is being talked about is: "Getting off the wall."

Glenn points out the advantages of puck possession time and directs Bo to enhance his ability to maintain puck control by getting his body away from the boards. This technique allows players to have room to cut back into ice that has been opened up as a result of getting off the wall. Secondly, this technique improves a player's ability to attack the net. (A tough thing to do when you are against the wall). This skill is being taught to a multi-million dollar paid hockey player who is thirsty to learn more.

This skill is unremarkable, but it is also extremely important. Ask yourself, at what age would learning this skill be appropriate? My guess is that Peewee would be a great time to learn and improve this skill.

Teaching body positioning to allow for excellent puck protection is a skill that becomes MORE and MORE valuable over time.

What it takes – Mental Toughness

It takes a lot.

Looking at an article in the Globe and Mail written by, Marty Klinkenberg, Connor McDavid was introduced to Brian Shaw, a sports psychologist who serves as an adviser to the Toronto Blue Jays. Shaw says:

"Like many elite athletes, McDavid is a perfectionist, which carries an emotional burden. Coping with defeat was especially difficult for him when he was younger, and often he agonized, feeling as if he had let his older teammates down." Shaw told McDavid, "it was not wrong to feel upset after a loss or a tough game, but that at a certain point he had to let it go."

Quinn Philips for Global News in his article – "the Anatomy of a Generational Player," Quinn quotes John Dunn, a University of Alberta sports psychologist – "Where superstar players like McDavid stand out, is in their brains."

Mr. Dunn's list of superstar psychological traits includes:

- Lack of fear of failure
- Commitment to train
- Attention to detail
- Ability to identify marginal gains
- Unwavering confidence and resilience

"They never ever lose that deep down belief that they are who they are and it's going to come back," Dunn said. "Whereas I think the rest of us, I don't think we've got that same unshakeable belief that they have in themselves."

Most importantly, according to Dunn, is passion.
"It fuels all the behaviors that are necessary to train, to commit, to make the sacrifice, to endure the hardship, to fuel the ability to rebound from disappointment," Dunn said.

Some chess players need 8x more practice to reach the expert performance as opposed to other players. The 10,000-hour rule should really be – between 4,000 and 40,000-hour rule. Mastering a skill is in all of us. Obsession is not.

And where Mr. Dunn opines that Connor McDavid stands out because of his brain – my thought is quite simple – it was that his brain was more talented. It was the hard work he put in every day to strengthen his brain to able to take in so much information – it still comes down to a crazy work ethic fueled by obsession.

I mentioned that not every player that utilizes a good skating/skills coach gets a free pass to the NHL and the reason lies here:

> Many players THINK they are obsessed. When they are NOT.

Many players THINK they are putting in the time just like their peers are. They are likely right. But if you polled the coaches to see how many have a shot at "pro hockey" or an "NCAA scholarship" – the poll would show that coaches understand that extremely few players have a "chance."

My point here is – if you think you are putting in the time, the SAME time that your peers are – you are likely 1,000's of hour's deficient from what CM and AM were able to do with their time as young, obsessed hockey players. And for that matter every player that receives an NCAA scholarship or CHL contract.

Multi-sport athletes

I am conflicted on the subject of promoting multi-sports to all of our hockey players. I played everything. Competive sports: soccer, long distance running, water-skiing, tennis, volleyball and playground sports: basketball, football, baseball and camp sports: sailing, windsurfing, canoeing, swimming. All formed my athletic makeup. For 99% of youth hockey players, playing other sports is a great way to become MORE athletic. Which in turn will help you develop more quickly at whichever sport you choose to specialize.

Except, more and more kids are specializing at a younger and younger age. And USA Hockey and Hockey Canada can't seem to stop early specializaiton. The train has left the station. They both try to point out the successful players who were multi-sport athletes growing up, but they NEVER point out the NHL players' that weren't mulit-sport athletes, like Connor McDavid.

Another perspective that USA Hockey and Hockey Canada seem to lose focus on is the fact that ALL of our hockey players do in fact play multi-sports. Five days a week, 3 times a day! That is, up until grade 8 (13 years old). All Canadians get two recess breaks each day for 15 minutes and about 45 minutes for a lunchtime break. My recess ended every single day with about a 90-second guzzle of water from the fountain as sweat poured down my forehead. We played everything: football, baseball, soccer, handball, basketball – 3 times per day, 5 days a week!

Connor McDavid didn't play other competitively organized sports, and Auston Matthews quit baseball at 13. He claimed he only liked to hit. Sounds about right for any action sport junky like hockey players.

But, in the absence of playing other high-level sports, they were both trained to become better athletes OFF the ice. Agility, running, catching, throwing, jumping, skipping, yoga, the list goes on and on and on. These players are incredible athletes, not just fantastic hockey players. And they both worked their asses off becoming better athletes OFF the ice. So if you don't play other sports, training off the ice is essential to becoming a better athlete and increasing your chance of going a lot further in hockey.

I wonder if the Brazilian soccer stars are encouraged by their Federation and coaches to quit soccer for 3-4 months every year in order to play other sports? Hmmm…I doubt it.

If we can agree that all around athletics is a key to reaching your potential in any single sport, then we must agree that our off-ice training must be focused on learning to become a better "mover" combined with enhancing a player's coordination skills. Can we do this? How? There is good news…the cost of the off-ice training comes at a fraction of our on-ice. If each player paid

$10 per workout session a season and teams had 50-75 off-ice workouts; it would cost an additional $500-750 per player. But that comes with the price of eliminating a sport from our routine, which may in fact turn out to be less expensive than playing a secondary sport.

This training comes at an expense – money. LOL. And we have all heard "if your son didn't play hockey, his University education would be 100% paid for with all the money we saved." True, but hockey is not about the destination, instead it's about the journey. And the journey in hockey is unlike any other sport. The training must become part of the fabric of who the player is. These stars do not look at training as a burden that must be overcome to achieve success. They look at it as another chance to perfect a skill or master an unlikely move. Imagine all the time and practice it would take to master a skill that might be employed once in 10 games. For every slick, cool move that we see on TV, I can assure you that it has been practiced – hundreds of times, if not thousands.

Teaching? Coaching? Maybe we should adopt the term -> "Teachers."

I want to round out this chapter that started by what Makes Connor McDavid and Auston Matthews so GOOD? They have an obsession to get better. And they used many different skills coaches to gain a competitive advantage over their peers. Attention to every detail was paid in full.

What's the difference between teachers and coaches? It is massive, and as a parent and player, you should be on the lookout for a teacher, not a coach, that is if you want to get better at hockey. If you want to win tournaments, find a good coach. Realize that you are a piece of a puzzle that is many times intended for the coach's success, not yours! Many coaches are praised for their "winning" success, and I don't think that will go away. And many coaches use their "winning" success to move themselves up the ladder into a more prestigious club, association, etc.

Look for a coach who does NOT want to move anywhere, that only wants his players to move upwards, that is committed to getting the most out of each individual player. To improve each player's chance of becoming an impact player. Ever met one of these coaches before? Unlikely. They are extremely rare, and the players that play for them never go looking for greener pastures. Of course, moving on is a probability for a coach like this, but putting your players first - ahead of the team success is a must for a great youth hockey coach.

Definition of "coach"
– One who instructs or trains, one who instructs players in the fundamentals of a sport and directs team strategy.
Definition of "teach"
– To cause to know something, to cause to know how to accustom to some action.

The most significant difference that I see above is that the skills coach (teacher) has the ability to finely detail the 4 skills of the game: Shooting, passing, skating and puck handling. On the other hand, most coaches instruct the drill and have little input on the details that go into excellent technique.

To become a remarkable coach you need to either learn how to teach these detailed techniques or have your team work in combination with a "skills" coach that specializes in teaching these techniques.

Hockey is becoming more like football – Head Coach, Special Teams Coach, Defensive Coordinator, Offensive Coordinator, Skills Coach, Goalie Coach and the list goes on. I think the term, Assistant Coach will slowly fade away and become one of the above. Specialized teaching.

"Today's secret is tomorrow's common knowledge. All you have to do is look."
- Anatoly Tarasov

Chapter 3

Coaching SECRETS

A hockey season is long. It is the requirement of a coach to keep the group fresh. Keep the group energized. Keep the group learning.

Too many coaches and parents define success by winning hockey games, hockey tournaments and league championships. To win at coaching, winning games should not be the barometer of success. Rather, adopting the principle of "developing MORE skilled players" is the definition of success. Individual improvements woven together to enhance the team is the key.

Why do coaches and parents put so much emphasis on wins?

As a parent are you looking at winning tournaments when you choose an organization for your son/daughter to play on?

League championships? For me, I am looking for the organization/coach that will help develop my son the most.

I want to share a short story about when I coached the Atom Oakville Rangers. I knew we already had a very strong team. And I wanted to clearly present the principle of "developing MORE skilled players" to the parents. I began our meeting with parents that happened soon after the team was selected. It started out like this, I stated, "A monkey can coach this team, and the team will only lose 5 games this season, my job is to coach this team and lose 10 games or more." The room went aghast. The parents wanted to go undefeated. I squashed that immediately.

The point that I got across to the parents is that winning games is not as important as improving. Becoming unafraid of making a skilled play in your defensive zone or playing the puck as a goalie in the last few minutes of a game defined who we were as a team. We lost many more than 5 games, but we continued to learn to play a skillful way. We never dumped the puck in. Our defense never rimmed the puck to the wingers. Our goalies roamed around outside the crease. That is development.

The season ended with our team playing a best of 5 OMHA finals against Cobourg, whose record was 66-0. We lost the first game and didn't lose another.

Coaching Secret #1: Season Breakdown

There are a few reminders to consider when looking at a hockey season:

1. Exhibition Games
2. Tournaments
3. Regular Season
4. Playoffs

1. Exhibition Games

These games are the best for instilling habits that have been developed in practice into a game.

The games also feature a "perfect" place for coaches to equal out ice time that may not be "so equal" in the BIG games. For example, coaches should be encouraged to play their "role" players into power-play situations. This is their chance to shine in an area that they normally might not play in. Role players should play WAY more minutes in exhibition games. Coaches should let the team and parents know that this is the way these exhibition games are going to be coached.

Exhibition games also allow players to experiment with creative concepts. Leaving the blueline to join an attack down low as a defenseman. Stepping up in the neutral zone. Breaking out with a pass to your partner in FRONT of your net. Goalies playing pucks that are "iffy." Joining the rush. Leading the rush as a defenseman. And generally playing a more RISKY game to see what the REWARDS could possibly be.

2. Tournaments.

Tournaments are like "mini" playoffs, but when they are treated like tests specifically aimed at players wanting to play a more vital role with the team – then the team will benefit hugely from teaching second line players to cope with the same pressures as first line players. To score and defend. Playoff success is often determined by your "depth" and the performance of the back half of your team. Remember this and train them for it. Tournaments are the perfect place to try players in different roles.

3. Regular Season

I look across both countries and wish that the regular season only sorted out the seeds for playoffs and DOES NOT eliminate any teams from the playoffs.

I think the Alliance Hockey Association (SW Ontario) does this particular trick very well. After an initial round robin set of games, the Alliance then splits each division into 2 divisions. Like A and AA. The top half of each division continue to play against each other for the remainder of the season and playoffs and the same goes for the bottom half. What is the point of winning or losing 10-0. Like I mentioned earlier, we all want a competitive challenge.

The particular reason that we ALL need to make the playoffs is quite simple – coaches can focus on skills instead of systems. And my bet will continue to be that if a coach spends enough time working on skills and his/her team has a low seed going into playoffs –the higher ranked team will not feel very good against this matchup.

4. Playoffs

Playoffs are most times formatted like a tournament. Top two teams may advance to provincials or states. Only in the OMHA to my knowledge, is there quarter, semi and finals all comprised of best of 5 playoff series for each round. Whether it is a tournament style or a best of 5 playoff series, coaches can now focus on winning.

Learning to win is a competitive advantage for life. But learning to win at the RIGHT moment might be the best advantage. Playoffs offer the right time to win.

Teams that have the most success in playoffs are the ones whose HABITS have formed over the season. Teaching is replaced with encouraging the behavior.

A part of the team will have to accept a different way to play. The "role" players must relish safety hockey. This part of the team spent an entire season working on skill plays – perfect. Now it is time to teach the role players to get pucks OUT and get pucks DEEP – this takes about one practice to learn. It also takes one practice to teach two players to forecheck and one player to stay responsibly high. Boom, your team is ready for playoffs.

As a coach, you can be proud that you spend 90% of the season working on "skilled plays" with the ENTIRE team and only in the playoffs will you adopt the role player approach to a part of your team.

Coaching Secret #2: Game Situations

There are many different situations that arise in a hockey game, but many of the following situations occur regularly enough to spend some time on addressing the situation and teaching players and coaches how to play in these. While I think the best method of training young players is "keep doing exactly what got you here," there remains some situations where changing the style of play is dictated by the scoreboard.

The aim of this next part of the book takes a closer look at the following situations:

1. Up by a goal
2. Down by a goal or two
3. Breakouts
4. Closing the Gap
5. Defensively Responsible – I don't think so.

1. UP by ONE

Your team is up by a goal with 5 minutes to play. What are the instructions typically given by a coach? Frequently, it is this: "Stop doing everything that got us to this lead." Become a dumb hockey player that is focused on one thing – don't let them score. I.e.:

- dump the puck in, no more turnovers
- only one forechecker or stop forechecking entirely (trap)
- goalie stay in the net (no more playing pucks)
- stop trying to make a good outlet pass -> get the puck out of our zone (off the glass)

This inevitably leads to the defense not skating up the ice on offense, which leads to poor gap, which leads to easy entries by the opponent, which leads to scoring chances on your goalie who is petrified to play the puck.

We have seen this collapse at every level of play, including the NHL. And here is the KICKER: The opposing team ties it up, and now the game has 5 more minutes and possibly overtime (playoffs). Now, what does the coach say to the team? "OK, now let's go back to playing hockey again." This is tough to do after the onslaught and momentum change.

So, why do we do this as coaches? It DOESN'T WORK! Stay away from fear and let the players play. Let the chips fall where they may, but my personal opinion is that its suicide to change the tactics that got you the one-goal lead when it is late in the game. Be positive and tell your players you believe in them.

Continue to force the opposition and continue to hunt for the NEXT goal. It is more rewarding and more successful!

2. Down by ONE (or two...sometimes three)

This is a frequent situation in all levels of hockey. At the pro level, players are constantly monitoring the risk/reward of every puck battle, pinch, hold the blueline, outnumber the opponent. These are a few of the situations that require a decision to be made.

Youth players and coaches already understand the risk tolerance of a game that is tied with lots of time on the clock – let's say the risk tolerance is 5/10. Right in the middle. I pinch when I think I can make it. BUT, youth players have a difficult time ramping this tolerance up to a 10/10, meaning that ALL situations are now calling for complete RISK and as a result players have to be comfortable giving up breakaways and 2 on 1's.

Keeping pucks in the offensive zone is the area where all players (5 or 6) must do everything in their power NOT to move backwards until a puck is flipped/bounced/banged into the neutral zone. Coaches must teach the subtlety of increasing the risk from 5/10 to 10/10 over the last minutes of a hockey game. If your team is down 1 goal, the tactic might be to wait until the final 5 minutes to start ramping up the RISK factor. But if your team is down by more than 1 goal, the coach will have to decide when to begin upping the risk. As coaches get good at this, there could be a double dip. This is when you raise the risk tolerance up and your team scores to lower the deficit to 1 goal. The coach may want the team to go back to the "standard" 5/10 risk tolerance for a while and then ramp it back up.

Remember, teams that are holding a lead are more likely to play a "protect the lead" style of hockey (risk tolerance 0/10), which can make for some tense minutes down the stretch as teams that can raise their RISK tolerance upwards signigicantly for a great chance at mounting come from behind wins.

3. Breakouts

Breakouts do not exist!

"What? There are tons of formations for breaking the puck out!" Yes there are, but here is the counter starting off with a question -> "When is the last time you saw two evenly matched teams playing against each other and the puck was dumped in with a forechecker or two chasing the puck and this happened: D1 retrieves the puck, passes to his partner, D2, behind the net, who moves the puck to the stationary winger at the hash marks, who moves the puck to the supporting center and away we go?" The answer is: it never happens.

Breakouts do exist when there are lopsided teams playing each other causing the weaker team to send a forecheck that does not amount to very much pressure. This gives the stronger team an opportunity to "breakout" the traditional way. However, the reality is that these lopsided games happen very infrequently.

So my point is simple – stop wasting time working on these plays. Yes, every player needs to know the basic plays, but don't worry about the execution. Instead, worry about learning to make a "skilled play." Evading a forechecker. Disguising the direction you intend to go. Faking a pass or rim. Then you have a team that can beat a forecheck and create a breakout by simply getting open and delivering good passes to each other. By the way, a great pass that is being employed more and more at higher levels is hitting the defenseman in front of your own net with a pass. We've come a long way – that pass used to be TABOO.

4. Closing the Gap

Closing the GAP – defense.

What is the expectation that a youth defenseman close the gap properly? ZERO. This is close to impossible.

To close the gap correctly, defenseman must learn the VERY FINE line where they can advance to before pivoting and accelerating backwards in order perfectly close the gap. This fine line takes YEARS to learn and here is a fundamental reason why coaches struggle to teach this: they get upset when an offensive player burns their defense wide or inside.

Coaches must learn one simple rule when teaching defense to close the gap (probably the most essential skill a defenseman has) – defenseman must be congratulated when they err on the side of closing too much gap leading to a breakaway or outnumbered attack. The idea here is straightforward: to learn to close the gap, a player will need to be burned 1,000 times. The faster you can get your players to get to the line OR PAST IT, the quicker they will figure out where the line is. Every time a defenseman backs up to accept a forward skating on them and DOES NOT have to pivot and accelerate to defend, always leads to a slower learning curve toward FINDING the correct line to close the gap to take 1,000s of attempts.

My rule of thumb is this: When defensemen are playing defense in one on one drills, the defenseman should get burnt 50% of the time. That is 50% more desperate pivots with desperate acceleration possible using the old fashioned stick on puck defensive play. This also allows the forward to drive wide, accelerate, cut in – rather than the usual lackluster effort because the defenseman just keeps backing in.

5. Defensively Responsible? Impossible.

Do I think we should teach how to be defensively responsible? – Yes. But, what is missing from youth hockey is teaching players how to score more goals. The reason is SIMPLE: most coaches can't teach players to score. They don't know how. But it is incumbent on coaches to spend no less than 70% of the training on offensive hockey specifically aimed at scoring more goals. Also, this is way more fun than learning how to play great positional hockey.

I also find this funny -> many youth coaches are bewildered when a defensive player goes into an area that is forbidden (an undisciplined move), yet I see this all the time in the pro level, especially the AHL. So, don't be heartbroken, it takes a long time to ingrain defensive responsibility in all situations. And my feeling is that this skill should be taught DURING games. When players come off the ice, grab the board, draw out the situation and use the mistake as a teaching moment. Getting out of place in practice is incredibly difficult to simulate, so use game moments for teaching this responsibility.

Instead of teaching defensive positioning, I wish more coaches would work on 2 on 2 and 3 v 3 in the low offensive zone. How to incorporate defense into a scissor cycle? How to recognize when a defensive player is off balance and explode towards the net. How to battle to generate a scoring chance. How to use your edges to maneuver away from a defending player and yet have the ability to have your head up to spot the open man.

Coaching Secret #3: Player Positions

<u>Defense</u>.

How do you know when to put a player on defense?

How do players get to their positions? Did some guru coach come and tell your 8 year old that he/she would be better on defense? Perhaps the young player is not scoring goals as a forward and a coach figures that defense is more suitable. Most young kids watch a hockey game and want to idolize the scorers of the game. The celebration. The group hug. Raising your stick in the air! I don't think too many kids say, "I want to be a defensive player." Every single "defensive" player in the NHL was a scorer in youth and junior hockey!

The more likely scenario goes something like this: "we need more defensemen, does anyone want to try it?"

But wait a minute. What if each team carried only 4 defenseman. Now there is a tougher decision to make. Play every 3rd shift or player every other shift...now the situation gets more interesting – more ice time. I am pretty sure Bobby Orr became a defenseman because he could play HALF (or more) of every game! I also bet that Bobby spent just as much time low in the offensive zone as he did low in the defensive zone!

So I want to remind coaches that have 6 defensemen on youth hockey teams the following: please allow your defense to play forward, ESPECIALLY during practices. And conversely, make your forwards accept a rush and learn some of the skills needed by a defenseman.

In general, for youth forwards to control the puck, they stick handle it, they play with it, they shoot it and pass it and play with the puck! YET our defense usually do the opposite; they rarely have the puck in practice, rarely shoot it and are taught to defend the forwards most of the time.

Coaches, review your practice plans and see if the defense is "handling" the puck and shooting the puck nearly as much as the forwards. Make the necessary changes to even this out.

The future of the game is to INVOLVE your defense up the ice. My rule is this: if a defenseman can beat one of his forward teammates up the ice, then the defenseman is allowed to become a forward for the rest of the shift, and that forward must fill in your defensive position. The reality is that this rule is rarely applied. I wish it would happen every shift.

The other thing I see in youth hockey is a scenario like this: the defenseman who joined the rush for an attack might have a decision to make. Do I continue to try to score? To go for a rebound? To stay at the crease to poke pucks in the net? To chase a loose puck to the corner? OR does trepidation enter the defenders mind? Does the instinct become to get back to your position?

Well if it is not apparent to you yet – have your defense pursue the puck and play a brief moment of forward <u>for the remainder of the time the puck is in the offensive zone</u>. Don't be so concerned with having a forward back on defense, because if this concerns you too much as a coach, then you haven't done your job allowing forwards to play just enough defense in order not to become a huge liability. A minor one, yes, but huge – NO.

Lastly, coaches, please have your defense learn both sides of the ice. There are some finer details in picking up pucks on your backhand and keeping the puck in the offensive zone on your "wrong" side. There should be comfort on both sides of the ice which comes from practicing pivoting both ways and constantly working on your weaker side.

Defenseman need to have the following skills to become great:

- Poise with puck under duress
- The mindset to make a play vs. get rid of the puck
- Excellent first pass
- Neutral zone gap control
- Defend thought – <u>Get puck</u> vs Deflect puck
- Ability to skate well enough to join the rush
- Ability to get open in the offensive zone and find the back door when appropriate (which in my mind is often)

Offense

A coach will want to win every hockey game – sure. However, what is more rewarding is seeing your team execute a play that you have been teaching. The hockey IQ just went up. That is the most rewarding feeling you get from youth level coaching.

Championships are for parents. I don't remember once going to school the next day and bragging about a tournament I won. That is for parents to do at work. Kids don't even post about it on their social media. It is just not that important. Parents on the other hand…never mind.

Coaches need to be more focused on skills attained and the plan to execute the skills in a competitive environment. We do way too many 2 on 1's in youth practice that are unlike a game because there is no back checker. Last time I looked, there were ALWAYS players chasing you down from behind with reckless abandon. How can we expect execution by consistently putting our players into this unrealistic environment? Yes, at first we need to teach it slower and what the puck carrier's options are and when to pass and when to shoot, but we ultimately need to place players into game environments to allow them to get used to the speed. More attempts, quicker decision making. This is offensive training.

Generate more offense by Seth Appert

Seth Appert is the head coach of the U.S. National Under-18 Team at the NTDP 2017/18 and here is what he says about developing: "Keep it. Keep it and share it with your teammates. Don't throw it off the glass, don't dump it in. I think youth hockey should almost have a no-dump rule. Dumping the puck should be treated with the same distain as taking a selfish penalty. I think defensemen whipping pucks off the glass or the boards instead of trying to make a tape-to-tape play should be viewed the same way. Mistakes should be encouraged. Taking calculated chances should be encouraged. When we have it, we don't want to give it up."
By Michael Caples

Wingers

Wingers need to be ready. Ready to help centers win pucks on faceoffs. Ready to get open in the defensive zone. Ready to take a hit to make a play. Ready to support the center up the ice. Ready to play down low if your center is the last player back. Ready to cover your point man. Ready to collapse low when the attack is low. Ready to block shots from the defense.

Wingers need a lot of versatility too, and many times I see youth hockey players get completely lost if they are asked to take a shift at the opposite wing or heaven forbid – center. Once again it is incumbent on parents and players to remind the coach to learn more than just RIGHT WING.

Attacking the left wing as a right shot is an entirely different view than streaking up the right wing as a right-hander. A player's vision is different, the puck position and possibilities are far more significant for a right-hander to come down the left wing. The middle opens up, a drive wide and tight turn puts you on your forehand and simply shooting the puck is better advantaged by coming down the left wing as a right-hander.

These details must be taught, and it should be the goal of every good youth hockey coach to be able to instantly switch your wingers and even appoint one to center without the player being lost on the ice. Who knows why some players end up on the wing and some on center. The classic response is that the centers need to be the best skaters or the smartest players. Hmmm...I'm not sure actually. However, I can tell you one thing – there is ONLY

ONE RESPONSE to this question from a potential Jr. Coach. "Son, I see that you can play left wing, but I want to see you play right wing – there could be a chance for you there." – ABSOLUTELY would be my response.

Wingers need to have the following skills to become great:

- Ability to take a hit to get the puck to the center
- Willingness to block shots (as if the players shooting were 3 years younger)
- Intensity on faceoffs, actively pursuing the opponent's ice and helping the center win EVERY faceoff
- Working hard to get open on regroups by coming back hard
- Forechecking with purpose
- Ability to read the probabilities of the opposing defensive breakouts

Centers

Centers must have the most awareness on the ice. The ability to see a winger that got sucked in low in the defensive zone and the acute awareness to fill his/her void as a winger until a switch can be made. Centers are like a 3rd defenseman that must be able to handle the offensive cycle and assist their defensive teammates in the recovery of pucks through puck battles all over the low end of the defensive zone.

Centers must possess uncanny vision, the ability to see late comers joining the attack and how to employ these teammates into an offensive rush. That is why most centers are extremely good passers – they have great VISION. Many times a creative center can stall with the puck, drawing defenders in and slowing the retreat of mobile defenseman, allowing the center to spot the streaking winger who now attains the advantage caused by the lack of speed of the opponent's defenders.

The centers who have the highest winning % for faceoffs are the centers that give 100% EFFORT EVERY faceoff. Believe me, it is way easier to put effort into the draw than to have to chase your opponent for the first 10 seconds of a lost draw. Getting low, getting intense, snarly, and approaching each faceoff as if the game depends on it are the abilities that separate many centers who win more faceoffs. Don't forget, the wingers play a massive role in the success of every faceoff – the team that is the most READY usually has an advantage.

The mindset has to be "totally determined." I sometimes tell my center – this is the mindset you need to have: "If you lose this faceoff, the opposing center gets to punch your mother in the face. Now, how hard will you try?"

Centers have to be great skaters (so does everyone else), but centers skate "more" than wingers do. They support the puck down low in the defensive zone, and they lead the attack from the middle of the ice.

Long gone are the days when wingers took a breakout pass and delivered a tape to tape pass to the center in great angling position in the middle of the ice. Wingers don't have time anymore for this pass, and usually this pass would result in the center having ZERO time with the puck as the defenders are no longer backing up in the neutral zone Instead good coaches have defenders moving towards the puck at all times. So this leads to centers gathering pucks that are chipped up the ice into free space in the neutral zone, creating footraces between defense and center to corral loose pucks. Should the defense win this race, the center's primary purpose is to take time away from this player and to hopefully create a neutral zone turnover – <u>it is the neutral zone turnover that leads to great offensive chances.</u>

Moreover, centers must be comfortable on both wings. I could never imagine getting passed over for making a team because I didn't have the necessary skills to move to another forward position. Instead of right wing, left wing and center – make sure you can play FORWARD.

Centers need to have the following skills to become great:

- Ability to SEE everything up and down the ice
- Willingness to battle down low to recover pucks and begin the offense
- Massive intensity on EVERY faceoff - get low, get angry, and put everything you have into winning every faceoff
- Creating neutral zone turnovers by putting on severe pressure to defending team's defense

- Ability to play EITHER wing, should the situation arise that two centers need to be on the ice (tie the game up, or a defensive zone faceoff late in a game) and
- Creativity to make plays to wingers and joining defenseman, finding a way to turn an even rush into an outnumbered rush

When I played in the DEL (Germany) my line with Rick Girard as the center became even more potent because of our faceoff success. Rick being left-handed took every draw on the left side of the ice (backhand), and I took all the draws on the right side of the ice. (Righty). We were both in the top 10 in faceoffs and over the course of a year, our team started every shift with about a 60% chance of having puck control. Way more fun!

Coaching Secret #4: INNOVATION

There are many factors involved in getting young players to develop quickly, which is the aim for most parents and coaches. To drill down a little bit, I want to explore four areas that will help coaches to develop young players at a faster rate:

1. Dump it in! – never.
2. Awareness
3. Fear NOT - coaching

4. Details

1. Dump it in! – never.

Rarely have I seen at advanced levels of hockey, Bantam to pro, where a clean breakout from defense to winger to center led to a golden scoring chance. More likely the center collects a puck and continues into offensive territory in the neutral zone, is confronted by the defense which leads to a dump into the offensive zone. This style of hockey is what I consider "Pro" hockey style. By dumping the puck, it accomplishes three things: 1) creates a race to a puck that is 200 feet from our net (a good thing);2) a good dump/chip results in a possible hit, turnover, and possession of the puck; 3) it eliminates a neutral zone turnover. Number 3 is the most critical component of advanced level hockey coaching, but here comes my 2 cents:

If you get PAID to play hockey, this is a no-brainer, continue to employ this tactic as evidenced by your coaches constant reminders!

If you DO NOT GET PAID to play hockey, use this technique as rarely as possible.

Instead, keep working on making plays. Figure out ways for 2 offensive players to attack a single defenseman on one side of the ice. Use creative cross and drops. Use a fake dump to grab a few tenths of a second. I am not a fan of going ONE on ONE all the time, but if forwards use change of speeds to put defense off balance – go for it. Or if you have been working on Connor McDavid's principle of accelerating through defense – go for it.

Youth hockey players and even junior hockey players must be given the right amount of leniency to practice making "OFFENSIVE" plays. A 'cross and drop' at the blueline, ability to push defenders away from the puck carrier with vision (the more you can see around you, the more leery the defense is willing to step up on you), inside drive and drop plays, stop and draw a hit to make a play, curl and find a late guy – these plays will get you NOTICED. Dumping the puck will NOT. Moreover, a note to coaches: please allow your less skilled players to have enough opportunities in practice to develop the skills necessary to become proficient enough to have less fear to try a "skilled play" in a game.

The dump, however, is the least skillful play in all of hockey. Save it for when people are paying to watch you play, and you have no other option but to listen to your coach. At these levels, wins matter!

I remember a story about when the puck controlling Russians arrived to the NHL and Slava Fetisov was coached by Scotty Bowman in Detroit. Scotty asked Fetisov to dump the puck in on a powerplay in practice, so Fetisov skates to the redline and fires a puck high into the empty seats of Joe Louis Arena. Scotty asks Fetisov why he did that to which Fetisov replies, "We don't have puck, then THEY don't have puck."

Not until all 5 Russian players joined Detroit to play together as a group did they begin to have the crazy, puck controlling success that they were known for. Scotty once said, "I coach the rest of the team, they coach themselves."

2. Awareness

There are times in every hockey game when players need to be more "mindful" of the game situation. It is the responsibility of coaches from U10 and on to teach situational training. For example, do all the players know the score of the game? If yes, do we know how much time is left in the period/game? Do we know if we are planning on pulling the goalie, or if the other team is planning this? Do we know when a penalty is about to expire? All of these situations can "change" the style of play **SLIGHTLY**.

In a situation where the goalie is about to be pulled for an extra attacker, does an offensive-minded player know this and perhaps choose a safer play knowing the goalie has or is about to be pulled?

Awareness shows up in tons of other areas. Have you ever seen a defender drop or break a stick? What tactic can be employed? Easy, attack the area of the defending zone where the player is stickless.

In a situation where your team is down by one goal, as a defender you have a choice to make a particular play – should I pinch or not? The situation presented usually does NOT call for a pinch, but if the defender does not pinch, the offense generates an easy attempt at an empty net that the defender has no way of covering. That should change the decision on whether to pinch or not.

There are tons of situations that call for AWARENESS and most of the time these situations are tied to the game clock and the score. Teach the scenarios. Teach the observations. Teach the slight change of tactics that are dictated by the particular situation.

3. Fear NOT – Coaching.

Fear coaching is very common among youth hockey coaches and it revolves around coaching against the "other" team. Fear of their offense. Fear of their defense. Fear of their power play. Fear of their best player. "Don't do that against this particular team."

When coaches preach about the "other" team, they insinuate that we need to stop them. I don't understand this. What about this instead? "They need to stop us." Coaches need to focus on their own team, rarely if ever talking about the opponent.

The mistake many coaches make is that their message to their team revolves around "the other team." And what I mean here is that instead of worrying about your own job and what you need to do to have a successful game, many coaches are sending information to their players about what "not" to do. This is coaching with fear. Try your best to steer clear of the fear. Put more concentration into YOUR team.

Keep the message consistent. Play your own game. Worry very little about the opponent.

Fear also manifests itself in other ways. For example, coaches often talk about: First shifts of periods, last shifts of a period and last two minutes of a game. These are frequent speeches. I totally disagree with all of these moments. Players must be encouraged to play the SAME for the entire hockey game, not just the 1st minute or last minute. A strong coach believes that there is no fear in playing the middle of the period the exact same way as the end of a period. Why change?

If players have been taught some "awareness", the speech about the last minute of the game is for kindergartners, and it is my opinion that EVERY shift matters and that the same work ethic and attention to detail goes into the first shift of the period as the 10th shift of the period. Expect nothing less.

However, if you align yourself with John Wooden, his pre-game speech amounts to pretty much – "let's go." The work has already been done in practice. It is just time to go execute.

4. Details.

Hockey is in the details. For example: does the flex in your stick meet the test of being able to generate 10cm of flex on every wrist shot? Details are in the details. Let's have a look at some of the details that I think are important to a youth hockey player's development curve:

- Do your players ASK why?

- Are ALL players cognitively engaged (focused and determined)?
- Is the staff keeping score for all "practice games?"
- Are players always thinking about body positioning (protecting the puck, angling the puck, in the shooting lane)?
- Preparation to play – putting practice habits into a game
- Communication between teammates on and off the ice
- Pursue your daily goals 100% of the time
- Watch hockey to get better
- Bring the most EFFORT every day
- Be a great teammate, an important life skill

10 Secrets of an INCREDIBLE Coach

Without a doubt John Wooden has impacted the way I coach. Learning his methodology and learning from his wisdom has helped me to become a better coach. So I do not take credit for the "10 Secrets of an INCREDIBLE Coach." These are from the Greatest Coach of ALL TIME (ESPN) - John Wooden:

1. **Belief**.

A good leader creates belief. Belief in the mission. Belief in collectively turning potential into incredible performance.

2. **Care**.

Look for ways to display that you care as a coach. Because if you care, you earn trust and with trust, you are enabled to lead.

"An effective leader is a good teacher – namely, how to perform at your highest level." Steve Jamison

"Hats of a coach – teacher, disciplinarian, role model, psychologist, motivator, timekeeper, referee, organizer. " Wooden

A great leader is a teacher who is a lifelong student." John Wooden. Learning is a lifetime pursuit.

Make the right kind of mistakes. Lose the right way. Win the right way.

3. **Create pride.**

Motivate using pride. *"A leader must have courage, including the courage to change."* Wooden

The best way to improve the team is to improve yourself. A good look in the mirror helps to reflect on the ENTIRE group, coaches included.

4. **Emotional control.**

If you cannot control your emotions, you become weak. Consider no motivating speeches, *for if your team relies on these workups to get excited to play, what have you done? Prize intensity and treat emotionalism as a weakness."* Wooden

If a coach loses control over his emotions, the gate is open for players and parents to lose their cool as well. Teams discipline always comes down to coaches emotional control.

5. <u>Valued.</u>

What does it mean to be valued? In anything you do, this is an essential feeling that gives meaning to the work you do. In all walks of life, there are many ingredients that go into a meal, and while the steak might be the feature, the rub, the cook, the side dishes are all part of the experience. In hockey the players are the steak, the coach is the cook, and the parents are the side dishes. The rub is the effort.

6. <u>Standards.</u>

Be relentless in your quest for ways to improve performance. Set standards that are higher than your peers. Dig into the details that are never small enough to be done correctly. The secret to success – a lot of little details done correctly.

7. <u>Time.</u>

Minutes. **Can you use time to get more out of a season than any coach around you?** Count up the practice minutes in a season. Make every minute count. Hockey is expensive, but it is crazy expensive if you don't respect the "minute."

8. <u>Preparation.</u>

How you practice is how you play. Mentally checked in. Give it your best, every time you lace up your skates. *"A leader's greatness is found in bringing out greatness in others. A robust exchange of ideas and opinions is healthy as long as it's done in a manner that is not disruptive."* Wooden

9. Winning.

"Winning was never mentioned at UCLA – never – only the effort, the preparation, doing what it takes to bring out your best in practice and games." Dave Meyers

10. Focus on EFFORT First

Focus on the effort not the outcome. Outcomes have success and failure and I think we can all agree that we learn a lot more from failure. Adversity. Without it sports becomes dull. How you deal with failure/adversity often determines future success. React to the hand you are dealt. Run with it, embrace it – for the challenge makes the sweetness spill out.

Coaching Secret #5: COACH & PLAYER Relationship

Once again, Mr. Wooden is able to perceptively articulate what the secret between a player and coach is.

John Wooden: "Master Coaching exists in the space between 2 people in the messy game of language, gesture, and expression.

Master Coaches can, by being so focused and by their deep knowledge of the subject, see and recognize the inarticulate stumbling, fumbling efforts of players reaching towards mastery, and then connect them with a targeted message.

Master Coaches are the delivery system for the signals and fuel which direct the growth of a given skill circuit, telling with excellent clarity to fire here and not here. Coaching is a long, intimate conversation, a series of signals and responses that move toward a shared goal. The subtle ability to locate the sweet spot on the edge of the player's ability, and to send the right signal to help the student reach toward the right goal OVER AND OVER.

Perceptiveness – it is all about figuring YOU out.

For me (Wooden) it is about seeking out the details of each athlete's personal lives, finding out about their school relationships, their anxieties, their personal goals, and struggles. A Master Coach has the quality of a confidante, a sounding board and a mentor for LIFE. The key is to connect with your player and to help your student understand your moral standards.

What makes YOU tick?

Part of a coaches role is to figure out what makes themselves tick.
Beyond teaching the game – coaches should aim for a higher purpose." John Wooden.

Never a single word about winning – the effort is what really matters.

No lengthy discussions – don't take more than 10 seconds to get your point across.

The bigger the game, the less speech is needed. Practices are for providing information; games are for displaying information. Wooden's 4 laws of learning – explanation, demonstration, imitation, and repetition with some added critique.

"If I can get the potential out of you – I have taught you to tap into your potential in anything you choose to do." Wooden

Coaching Secret #6: Practice

Practice Planning – areas to consider:
A. Warmup. Games and Practice.
B. Skills (learning the skill)
C. Game Situations (applying the skill)
D. Example – Outnumbered Rushes
   (2 on 1 both sides of the puck and 3 on 2's)
E. Example – Defensive Zone Coverage
F. Shaping Practice

A. Warmup. GAMES and PRACTICE.

In games, most youth teams only get 3 minutes to warm up. And sometimes by the time the team is actually on the ice, the clock has already ticked down to 2:30. Not much time to do anything – without a GREAT plan. As we get older, (U16 and above) players finally get 5 minutes to warm up. Still, a GREAT plan is needed to get the team feeling good going into the game.

In practice, the coach decides how long is necessary to get the team loose and ready to go. Just taking a quick BET by my readers – how long do you think I spend warming my team up before practice? Answer – zero minutes. We start practice right away. Our team adopts the "no minute wasted program."

But, what exactly is the purpose of a warmup? Anything over 6 minutes is 10% or more of the practice. Do your players stretch on the ice at practice? If they do, do they also do it in a game? It seems to me that that piece should be consistent. It is unlikely though because of the short timeframe allocated to warmups in a game. My rule of thumb is that if you stretch, do it before going on the ice. There is absolutely NO evidence that stretching reduces the likeliness of injury.

What about the goalie?

Is the intent of a warmup to get the goalie ready? Hmmm…at any age group, this can be accomplished with 1 or 2 players shooting at the goalie and/or backup goalie.

Is the intent to warmup our shot? I personally don't think so.

The hardest part of youth hockey is - passing. There are so many variables to connecting a good pass. Speed, direction, distance all measured in a blink of an eye. This is the most crucial part. A few "game like" passes would help players immensely.

The worst drill in all of hockey – the horseshoe – needs to be eliminated from every team, everywhere and here is why: The drill features one player moving and 14 players standing still. A player begins by skating from one corner out towards the neutral zone and turns back to accept a pass from the player in the opposite corner. This pass can literally be passed blindly into the neutral zone, no measurement of speed is required, no measurement of accuracy is needed at all because the player that is accepting the pass will alter the skating route to ensure that the pass connects. As I like to say, "my grandma could make that pass."

Warm-Up Drill for Practice

Here is a warmup drill that I use – it accomplishes a ton of different things:

A drill where the coach starts in the middle of the blueline with a bunch of pucks. Dump a puck into the goalie to play to his left. A defenseman picks it up, winger skates down the dots, then skates laterally to the hash marks, receives a pass, connects to a center that mirrored the defense (but not as deep). The 2 forwards cross and drop in the neutral zone, reattack same end, outside shot.

Add-on: Defense 2 picks up a puck and skates laterally along the blueline, back and forth waiting for the two forwards to stop at the net. Point shot. Rebound. Tie up one F in front.

Then Defense 2 sprints towards the goalie who has now played a puck to his right (dumped in by the coach, direct or rim) and the drill continues on the other side.

This drill has so many GREAT points of emphasis:

- Game like retrieval of puck by defenseman; can work on 3 hard strides backwards, with a pivot and communication with goalie
- Forwards sprint back low to become good options of D with great targets, accept pass and work on burst of speed to redline, cross and drop or work on a fake drop pass, drive net 2 on 1, get shot from outside, rebound, point shot, tip / deflection, D tie up one F in front

Make Hockey Great Again

Bantam   Length: 60 mins   Number of Players: 16-20

Equipment: x cones, x tires, x border pads, x nets

Drill Name: Practice Warmup

This drill is to quickly warmup:
Emphasis: passing, shooting, decision-making, goalie setting up pucks for defense, gap control, pivots, fake drop pass, NZ speed, wide shot, drive crease, tie up forward

Coach – shoots the puck from center ice to goalie, goalie must set up puck to his left (then his right with next puck) for defense to retrieve puck.
D1 – must make 3 hard strides and pivot to chase puck.
D1 – can get back of net (stop) or tight turn or wheel to open corner and hit either W or C.

Once pass has been made, Wing and Center exchange puck and speed towards redline for cross and drop or fake the drop.
W and C attack the D1 - 2 on 1 from half ice.
*** Coach can play next puck to goaltender once W and C receive pass from D1 on breakout.

Note: *6 players can be going at the same time in BOTH ends. 12 players moving.*

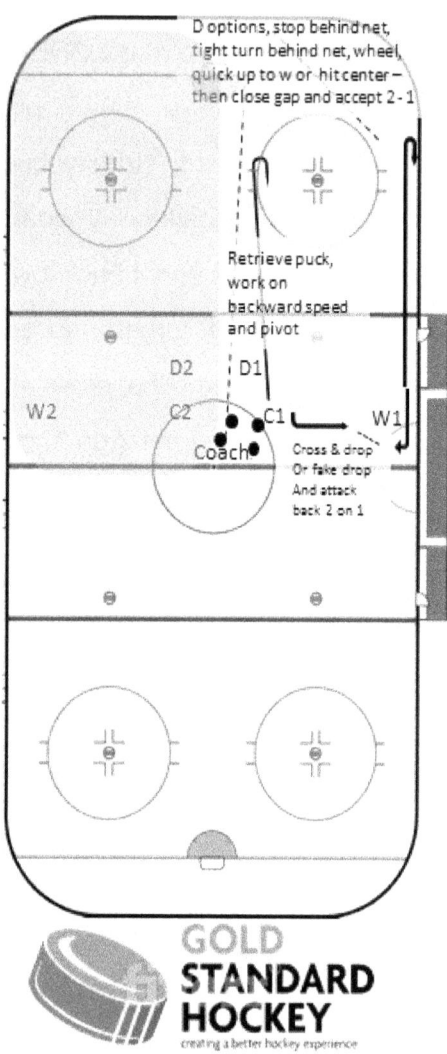

It is important to alternate sides of the ice. To keep this drill going with some pace, and to keep 6 players moving at all times, it is critical to the player's attention to the next puck being played by the goalie. The goalie will always alternate sides to deflect the puck towards.

Next, the coach will shoot the puck towards the goalie to play to his left, and the timing of the next puck being played by the next 3 players will be about the same time that the first group is heading towards the cross and drop in the neutral zone.

3 more players begin to breakout on the other side of the rink. If you have full-ice, you can do this drill in all 4 corners. 12 players moving at the same time. The assistant coach is running the other end. 12 players are moving at once. Now that is a warmup. Game situation all the way.

There are endless variations to this warmup: the way the puck is shot in, the defense can "wheel," the defense can escape, the defense can hit the center, the defense can join the attack for a "late man" chance, the defense can close the gap and pivot to backwards and play the 2 on 1. The defense can scissor or high roller off the blueline instead of shooting.

Game Warm-up Drill

I like to have every player put a puck in their bottom hand of their glove BEFORE they go onto the ice. Players should sprint onto the ice as if they have been shot out of a cannon, get their legs moving, get the blood flowing and heart pumping. After a lap or two, players can slow down, drop the puck and practice puck handling and edges. Continuing in a Nascar circuit, players must use the next lap to work on fakes, curls, head up, pivots, all warmed up at a slower speed. Players finish the fast/slow laps by shooting a wrist shot at the goalie skating down the middle of the rink. Once each shot has taken place, players alternate into each corner, with the team divided in half, standing in each corner – eerily similar to the horseshoe right! LOL.

The next part involves the back and front of each line in the corner. The back of each line is reserved for the defense, the front of each line for the forwards. Line #1, back player skates behind the net (or in front) and hits Line #2 forward with a pass. (The defense can also hit the F1 coming across the middle like a center) Both forward players skate towards center and cross and drop in the neutral zone. The puck is finally moved to the "outside" player, and a shot is taken from the top of the circle with the middle player going to the net for a rebound. This quick 2-1 regroup is done on HALF ice.

This drill takes practice and ALERTNESS – because <u>the next group GOES as soon as the forwards begin their cross and drop</u> at center. Which means that the defense player of Line #2, must be ready to head towards the back of the net when the two forward players are crossing at center. Younger age groups tend to fall asleep and forget to begin the other side. When done correctly at least 6 players are going at the same time. These passes are "game-like" because they represent a breakout type of pass. Options are available. The forwards make up to 3 passes. There is an outside shot (game-like, I don't see too many wicked wristers from the slot in a game) and there is a middle drive player looking for rebounds, which helps keep the goalie focused on preventing rebounds.

This Game Warmup has many points of emphasis:

- D accelerating to bottom of circle from corner, pivot to backwards, pivot to forwards, cut in front or behind net, look for 2 options - #1, winger and #2, center
- F show great targets and once received pass – burst of acceleration up ice and move puck to each other
- F work on cross and drop or fake the drop, and accelerate towards D on a 2 on 1
- Use outside shot and net drive

Add-ons:

D1 and D2 move out of corner at the same time (eye contact is key) and D1 can perform a reverse or a D to D behind net, or a D to D in front of the net.

After either D to D play, defense will move puck to any F. New player must join this drill – F3. So all three F are options for passes from D, and the F's regroup in neutral zone for a quick 3 on 2 attack.

OR

On regroup, D that did NOT pass puck to forwards collects another puck in the corner and works their way to the blueline, handling puck laterally along blueline waiting for Forwards to complete the 3 on 1 rush attempt. D shoots with traffic for tips and deflections. Next 2 defense begin. 5 players going at all times!

Peewee   Length: game   Number of Players: 16-20

Equipment: x cones, x tires, x border pads, x nets

Drill Name: GAME Warmup

This drill is to quickly warmup in a situation that is similar to what will happen in a game (moments away):
Emphasis: passing, shooting, decision-making, goalie setting up pucks for defense, gap control, pivots, fake drop pass, NZ speed, wide shot, drive crease, tie up forward

D1 – begins with a short skate to bottom of circle and pivots to backward skating – decision-making time – go around back of net, or in front of net
D1 – pass to either F1 player. (Winger or Center)

F1's – must regroup on HALF ice, same half as pass is made towards.

Once either F1 has received puck, D2 begins

Addons:
D1 and D2 work together – move out of corner and backskate together – they can use reverse if they want or D to D in front or behind net.
Make pass to either F1, add third F to become center and support the play, regroup 3 v 2, speed in NZ, wide shot, drive net, rebound.

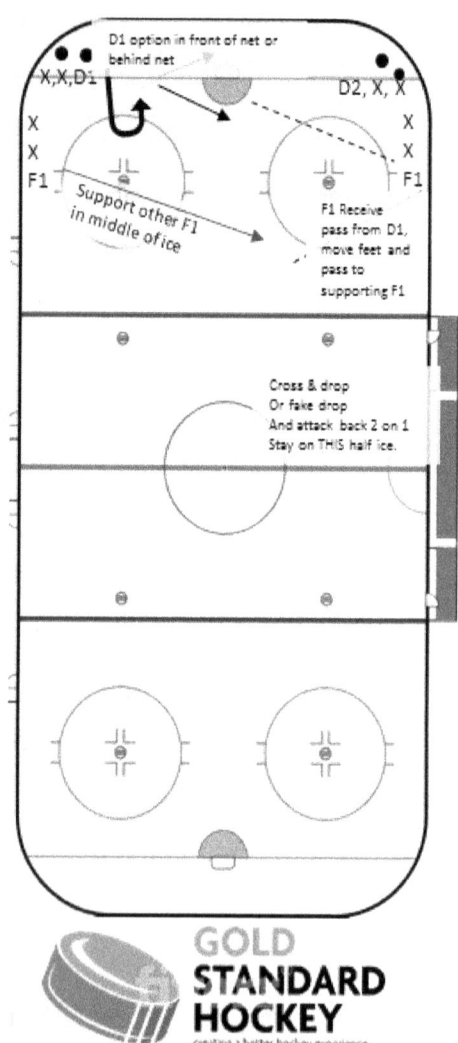

B. Skills – learning the skill

I want you (the reader) to think about the skill: Learning to shoot the puck. You hire a shooting coach. Your son or daughter receives scores of lessons and the techniques of shooting and the multitudes of practicing really begins to pay off – the shot is becoming stronger, quicker and more accurate – IN PRACTICE! The skill of shooting has been improved in an environment that is the exact opposite as that of a game, where time is NOT important, where game-sense is stymied because shooting the puck involves getting into position to shoot the puck with defenders all over you.

If you want to work on shooting the puck, the shooting coach should be blocking you from accomplishing the task – every single time. Players must learn how to overcome the BLOCK in order to get a shot off. Shooting the puck brilliantly has many, many more complexities than the technique of firing the puck.

It is an incredibly difficult task to accomplish in a game. "While it is convenient to separate game sense and technical ability in practice, there is a continual interaction among technique, tactics, and strategy in sports." Play Practice. And what Alan Launder is talking about here is that the technical ability MUST be learned in the exact same environment that its application is intended for.

So, in order to really become a better shooter, the situation of shooting must always be mimicked by a game feel, where defenders are closing on the player and the time required to shoot is continuously evaporating.

Have you ever watched a YouTube hockey coach? A sensational puck handler like Pavel Barber? He is an extremely gifted puck handler, almost magic hands. And I think that by following him, players will benefit tremendously. But I also think that players and parents must continually try learning skills that are as similar to the game environment as possible. Check out and follow – pavelbarber.com.

While perfecting skills in practice without forcing decisions and problem solving can be significantly improved in practice, these skills have an increasingly more difficult path to show up in the game. It's because players lack the ability to problem solve in the game environment. Players and parents should always look at a skills coach and ask – are we practicing in a situation that is fast and difficult like a game? If so, players will speed up the development of the skill like an Ovechkin one timer.

Let's take a look at an incredible youth hockey player. A team of experts came to his practice and used lasers and radar guns to measure the team's abilities. This incredible player's ratings are off the charts. This player measured:

Shooting ability – 10/10

Passing ability - 10/10

Skating ability 10/10

Puck Handling ability 10/10

What you have here is the next Connor McDavid, right? WRONG. What you have here is a player that should win each event at the NHL all-star game competition.

So if you have a player that measured a 10/10 shot, we have all seen the defenseman with a killer slap shot that uses it once every 15 games. It is an extremely difficult shot to get off with power. It takes time to wind and fire and there is pressure coming at you from all angles! Think about this for a moment – there are 3 HUGE skills a player needs to shoot a puck well in a GAME. 1. Ability to skate, mobility to move laterally, finding time to release the puck. 2. Ability to deceive, finding more time to release the puck. 3. Ability to shoot.

Think about how much better your players would get at shooting if – EVERY TIME THEY SHOT THE PUCK THEY WERE CONFRONTED BY AN OPPONENT. Once the essential skill is learned – ie. How to shoot a puck, the next step is to always confront the shooter. Let the shooter figure out how to skillfully get the shot onto the net – in a hurry! Moreover, if players are not confronted, how can we as coaches get the players to behave as if they were confronted? Don't just shoot the puck, make a move and shoot the puck – every time! Pull and shoot, push and shoot, fake and shoot. All part of the repertoire of an elite shooter.

See, the skills have to be tied to the game. And as the game gets faster and faster, the skills must be able to keep up with a defender whose main objective is stopping you.

Puck handling through cones, stationary shooting at targets, and skating a fast lap around the rink – don't really add up to much. Instead, coaches need to look at ways to enhance player's puck handling skills by providing random obstacles -> like players defending!!!

When learning a skill, the environment must be altered to let the player have enough time to set in motion the technique to be mastered. Mastering the technique is not critical. What is critical is learning the skill in an environment that mimics the environment that the skill is needed – the GAME.

C. Game Situations applying the skill – time becomes CRITICAL.

Where game-sense can be enhanced: The ability to understand the situation, and to make a decision to execute a particular skill while under duress. The mastering of the skill will come to the player faster if the player is put into a game-situation that makes the player understand (cognitive) and execute (athletic).

Coaches must understand that "realistic practice scenarios that can simulate the demands of high-level competition while retaining the crucial element of play is a more enjoyable process by all players," says Alan Launder in his book, Play Practice

Remember, under game-like scenarios there is so much going on in an athlete's mind: what skill to use (data retrieval), what information has been gathered (can I chunk this scenario together from past experiences), interpretation(mapping of 9 other players 360 degrees around you), and execution; all wrapped together they begin to form Hockey Sense. Without this type of decision mode training, we might as well have all-star competitions instead of hockey games.

D. Outnumbered Rushes

When we look at practice and begin to shape our situations that mimic games, players and coaches will find the training experience to be more rewarding. (Notice how I did not say "drills"). Let's take a closer look at the 2 on 1 situation. An excellent scoring chance for older players, but if you took my Coach Quiz from Chapter 4, you would know that even this outnumbered rush doesn't result in very many goals. The reason – execution. Seeing the variables. Understanding the possibilities.

We practice 2 on 1's all the time, right? However, what we do not often put in the drill is adding a backchecker. Moreover, I have not seen too many outnumbered rushes in a game WITHOUT a backchecker.

I believe that if we do not put pressure on the forwards from the backchecker – we are actually suppressing learning to execute a well-crafted scoring chance. When too much time is given to forwards (never really an option in a game), defenders begin to back up too much because they have no support from the backchecker. Speed is no longer valuable. Both forwards and defense are learning an irrelevant skill. The decision-making skills (hockey sense) can only be built by keeping the players in game mode using game speed with players learning from situations in practice that resemble a game.

Increase Execution for 2 on 1's.

To begin with, I want to ask if coaches and parents understand what the STRONG side is? Moreover, what the WEAK side is? This is an older term that coaches used to describe a player on a particular SIDE of the ice. The strong side is -> a right handed player on the right side of the ice. The weak side is -> a left-handed player on the right side of the ice. Therefore, a strong to strong 2 on 1 involves a right-handed player with the puck skating on the right wing and a left-handed player getting open to receive a pass on the left wing.

It is crucial to understand what is happening during a 2 on 1. There are 8 different scenarios. Well, four really, then they are mirrored on the other side of the ice.

So let's take a look at just the RIGHT side of the ice. The scenario on RIGHT WING with the puck has 4 different looks, remember you can be playing RIGHT WING as a lefty:

1. Right-handed with the puck, to lefty getting open
2. Right-handed with the puck, to righty getting open
3. Left-handed with the puck, to lefty getting open
4. Left-handed with the puck, to righty getting open – my favorite for scoring goals.

The scenario of LEFT WING is reversed.

So every 2 on 1 has eight different variables. Each variable has many different solutions. It is too much to teach young kids what the options are for each scenario all at once. So try breaking up the scenarios. Consider Strong to Strong and Strong to Weak. Learn the possibilities of these TWO situations.

Each of the above situations will eventually become clearer to players as to what options lead to the most success for each scenario. The success rate will change slightly from player to player, but my personal opinion is: In scenario #1, the right-hander with the puck has a better chance of scoring if he shoots the puck. Over time, the right-handed player will learn that the pass to the left handed player leads to dismal scoring efficiency. I think that scenario #2 and #4 are the best for passing. And like I mentioned above, when I get a chance like scenario #4 (my favourite), it is because the puck is in the middle of the ice, and I have a great angle to shoot, a more accessible pass to a lefty for a one-timer, and if I get in too close, I still think I can deke the goalie.

On offense, players should be learning how to disguise the puck position, learn the ability to quickly change the puck position between shooting and passing positions. Use eye fakes to fool the defense and goalie. Understand which situations are best for shooting and which are best for passing -> the most critical factor for development is when the players figure this out on their own.

Defending the 2 on 1

It is just as critical to teach defenseman how to defend these situations. At higher levels, defensemen must learn which situation is best suited for sliding or attacking the puck carrier, or noticing that the open player has NOT adjusted to a scoring solution, which means a defender can attack the puck carrier.

The defense can learn to read the eyes of the offensive player. Can you pretend to give the shooter the "shot" and then quickly take it away? Can the defender notice the puck position – is the puck in a shooting or passing position?

If you ever notice high caliber defenseman who challenges the puck carrier sometimes and other times he doesn't. Why? If you ask the defenseman 9/10 times he doesn't know the answer either. But the reality is this: they don't know exactly why they do what they do, but their subconscious and experience bank take over.

The 3 on 2 – Creating Offense from this rush

Let's face it, a 3 on 2 is not a great scoring opportunity for players of any age group including junior. It can be taught, however, to be an opportunity for a rebound, a tip/deflection and a goal scored by players that want to go to the "hard" areas of the ice. Namely, the crease.

When a 3 on 2 drill does NOT have a backchecker, passing to the "high" guy becomes the most acceptable play. (However, as mentioned earlier, this play is irrelevant because the "high" guy is caught most times in a game by the backchecker). By passing the puck to the "high" player, we have created a false environment that is opposite of what our intentions were. The intention, of course, being to become more productive at 3 on 2's.

Unless there is a massive gap between the 3 on 2 and the backchecker, the option to pass to the high guy will almost always be met with interference from the backchecker. So this pass should be banned.

Instead, both players without the puck should be encouraged to go to the net. Ready for rebounds and tips. Skillful players can manipulate the defense and use slippery passes (between defenders stick and feet) to players driving the net. Try turning a 3 on 2 into a 2 on 1. A skillful puck handler will let the defense attack and make a 5-10 foot skill pass to teammates who have not decelerated. When you add in the backchecker, you get – middle drive, speed on the outside, attempts to the top of the crease. Passes across the Royal Road for the older players. Speed on the entry.

E. Example #2: Defensive Zone Coverage

Any coach knows that a massive piece of empowering a team to win hockey games starts with being able to defend your own end. Many coaches spend too much time covering this area. This is a big part of the game, but the reality is that this is one of the easier pieces of teaching hockey. The players will learn how to position themselves to play strong defensively. Coaches will break down scenarios – if the puck is in this particular area, then I want our defense structured "like this." And so on, and so on...you get the idea. This is what I call "perfect world defense." The coach moves about the ice with the puck and the defense shifts accordingly. Easy eh? Until the real action begins and players get sucked into moving "out of position." This happens right up into the NHL. Offensive players are trying their best to manipulate the defense into making POOR decisions.

To counter the "perfect world defense" coaches should be encouraged to teach defensive coverage by learning how to create smaller games, inside the game.

Teach the concept. What are we as a group trying to do? And most critically, if one of our defenders gets beat -> how will the rest of our team react to counter this blunder?

The best way to teach defensive zone coverage is to introduce the concept of defending from the middle of the ice. Keeping offensive players to the outside, positioning the defenders between the offensive player and the goaltender.

To practice this concept, consider breaking up the 5 on 5 play and practice 3 on 3. To do this, put 2 offensive players low on one side of the ice with their partner defenseman on the blueline. Now place the 3 defenders. 1 defenseman low, 1 forward low, (covering the 2 offensive players low) and 1 forward high (covering the defenseman). Game situation. Let the play begin. The concept can be that if a defender low gets beat, the high defender collapses to help.

This situation gets trickier for the high defender. In a real game, this would be a winger covering their point man. Where it gets tricky is when the defense leaves the blueline – joins the players in the corner or goes to the front of the net. This was an uncommon play just 5 years ago, but in today's game, defenseman don't camp out on the blueline for very long. Defenseman are scissoring down the boards or high rolling into the slot and heading to the net.

The offense has changed. So too must the defense. Coaches must take a man on man approach to defending this type of offense. Otherwise, the high defender (winger) will be left covering -> nobody.

To further achieve working on defensive zone coverage, coaches must confine the space. It becomes more difficult for the offense, but it simulates the game, which is the key.

Defenders need to learn to defend with their feet. Defenders must learn not to over-defend putting yourself behind or even beside the offensive player.

- Consider 3 defenders with no sticks. Then 1 stick, then 2 sticks
- Consider 3 sticks upside down. Then 2 sticks upside down Then 1 stick upside down – any combination of these scenarios will help teach defending.

The real key to defending is to be able to defend without needing to use your stick. The abilities to close gaps, the agility to stop and turn using your body to direct the offensive player, cutting the offensive player off without ever letting the offensive player on the inside of the ice.

Learning D zone coverage is excellent for learning how to create more offense too. Offensive players should be focusing on attacking the weakest player (the player that has no stick, or the player with their stick upside down), learning how to interfere with the defense, forcing switches as much as possible. Learning how to "get off the boards" and get to the inside of the ice using fakes, (fake stops, fake turns, acceleration) drawing defenders close to our hips and manipulating a defender by giving "false" information.

Toss in the garbage (the former way to coach defense), and play game situations where coaches can manipulate the rules to achieve the desired effect.

Note: when the defenders recover the puck from the offensive players, my rule is always this: the defending team must skate and/or pass the puck to another defender and skate the puck out of the defensive area. The reaction between defending and then winning the puck to transitioning from defending to offense is a crucial component of skilled playing. Ensure that you work on this transition!

F. Shaping Practice.

As you learn to shape practice to become more realistic to game situations and worry less about the precision or execution, you should also consider letting the drill play out for a few seconds.

Good habits start with trying to find a solution – and when failure arrives – accessing the decision-making skills to determine the next move will become a habit.

The access to these moves is called chunking. Using experience to find a reliable solution. In hockey, we chunk a lot by learning what is the next move, when (if) this move fails. Good hockey players are always thinking about failure and how to turn failure into a positive. Missing a 2 on 1 doesn't mean the drill is over, what is next? How do we add on to this drill by continuing to figure out our next move? What does the defender do? Shooter? Passer? What are the moves for the next player joining the attack and the next player defending the attack?

Once you are able to shape practice, I would consider doing the SAME EXACT PLAN twice in a row. The first time, players are learning the expectations of the drill, and the second time through, players can focus on the execution of the skills.

Coaching Secret #7: PREPARATION

Preparing your team for a season full of success involves a ton of planning. To prepare coaches and associations better, I started a company called Gold Standard Hockey. GSH takes aim at using a timeline that addresses when certain items will be addressed by both the Head Coach and the Association/Hockey

Director. The other concept of GSH is to streamline the ease for both the Head Coach and Hockey Director to keep aligned and assure that the season is a complete success. If you are interested in a more in depth look at the ELITE preparation for a successful hockey season, please visit: goldstandardhockey.com

The timeline is altered somewhat because of the different dates for tryouts (May vs. August/September) depending on where you live.

In my lap around the USA and Canada, tryouts are typically held right after the hockey season, typically in May. It is a fair time to assess the players because everyone has just finished the season. Up until U15, I am a big fan of this timing for tryouts. Because teams are formed in May, it lets the Under 14 DOB players go play other sports without worrying about tryouts in late August / early September. This also fights off the "Smiths" who put their kids in hockey all spring/summer long to get a step up on the rest of the players, which happens all too often when tryouts are scheduled in late August / September. It is without a doubt that the Smith kids will have an advantage come tryouts in August / September but from my experience that advantage usually fades away 4 weeks into the season.

For the players that are older 15+, for competitive players spring/summer becomes part of a year round training, and these players should take a month off after the season and begin training hard all summer to come to tryouts in peak performance and conditioning. Also, there tends to be more movement in these midget divisions as some players are trying to move on to Jr. A or Major Junior clubs (confusing eh? Here is the difference: Jr. A is where Canadian players play to get NCAA scholarships and Major Junior is the conglomeration of our top 3 Major Junior Leagues across Canada, namely: WHL, OHL and QJMHL where the major focus is on developing players to play pro hockey. The top junior programs in the United States are the USHL and NAHL where these two leagues provide the 95% of NCAA scholarships awarded – the top College Hockey programs in the U.S. are monitoring every player in these Canadian Jr. A and the two U.S. junior leagues.)

In Calgary, where tryouts for all ages are typically held in late August / early September, there are lots of hockey businesses that generate a ton of interest because of the fear of losing ground to the Smith family. And the possibility of their child "not making the team."

Because most of Canada and the entire USA (exception Prep schools) conduct tryouts in May, I will begin this timeline at the moment when the coach accepts the positon as Head Coach, usually in February and as early as December of the season prior.

I have underlined the areas that I will go into more depth. These key areas bleed into what preparation needs to become:

Prior to Tryouts:
1. February/March - Head Coach accepts the position and attached Job Description (see www.goldstandardhockey.com

which outlines the duties of the Head Coach and is shared with parents and players.

2. February/March – Head Coach puts together a Season Plan. This plan should serve a dual purpose – to ensure that the plan fits the Association's philosophy and secondly to communicate to parents the expectations for the upcoming season.

Post Tryouts

3. June/July – Divide Season Plan into Block Plans that help keep the development of individual and team concepts on track.
4. August – Set coaching goals for the team and share with the Association
5. August – Team Bonding and Parent Bonding excursion
6. September – Player Goal Setting (see Chapter: Champion Goal Setting.)
7. October/November – Participate in Coach Development
8. December – Player Evaluation Meetings with Parents - present and review of Player Goal Setting
9. January – Coach Self-Assessment of season
10. January – Player and Parent Feedback to Association
11. February – Coach Performance Review – rehire

Head Coach Job Description

The idea of a 50 point inspection of the Head Coach's job is to keep everyone accountable to the process of the best way to develop young athletes both on and off the ice. This inspection list should be scrutinized every year and it should continue to shift and align with the culture of the Association.

Being a Head Hockey coach for a youth team is a huge challenge, and the principal challenge is that the parents become entwined deeply in the team's success and failure. I love the transparency of the inspection list, the parents job description should be 50 points as well!

Let's dig in and look at what the job actually entails:

Essential OFF ICE Responsibilities:
1. Review and become compliant with Association Policies and Rules
2. Update a *Season Plan* for specific age group (template provided by Association)
3. Tournament selections (in accordance with the Season Plan)
4. Oversee team budget slush fund and operate team within guidelines previously committed to in the Season Plan
5. Prepare age appropriate Summer Plan
6. Prepare *Season Goals* (template provided by Association)
7. Prepare a *Coach self-assessment* for the Association in December
8. Involvement in professional development at off-ice coach meetings
9. Plan on and off-ice hockey-related activities as outlined in Season Plan
10. Effective use of video training or other technology to enhance player development (conference room) outlined in Season Plan
11. Integration of sport psychology outlined in

Season Plan

12. Supervise and direct assistant coaches, assign duties as required
13. Provide leadership to ensure that the Association is maintaining the athlete code of conduct, coach code of conduct and parent code of conduct
14. Adjust coaching techniques based on the strengths and weaknesses of athletes.
15. Recommend hockey-related activities, home skills training, clinics, skill-improvement courses, and pre-season training camp
16. Evaluate individual athletes' off-ice strength and conditioning - review performance to determine path for improvement of their fitness strength and cardio
17. Demonstrate commitment to players' success and ability to improve each athlete by implementing evaluation tools. *Player Evaluation meeting* with coaches, athletes and parents to take place in December
18. Excellent interpersonal communication skills and the ability to work effectively with young athletes, team coaches, parents, and hockey executives.
19. Demonstrate ability to work through conflict situations effectively, (use of 24 hour rule and team liaison.)
20. In-charge of the team bench & locker room during games & practices.
21. *Player Goal Setting* - Build athletes confidence by working with them to create short and long term goals
22. Develop positive personal relationships with each athlete. Respect and understanding play key roles in this aspect of coaching effectively. Plan on and off-ice hockey-related activities in consultation with the Association.
23. Effective use of Manager for all communication to

the team

Essential ON ICE Practice and Game Responsibilities:

24. Coordinate the selection of Players at Tryouts
25. Coordinate the selection of Captain and assistant Captains, and provide a leadership plan for the entire team. Come up with the "Messier" plan.
26. Use *Block Plans* to effectively manage the development of an entire season.
27. Pre-Plan, organize, and conduct practice sessions.
28. Practice plans and pre-competition routines are specific, detail oriented and demonstrate overall purpose
29. Effective use of small area games to accomplish game-like situations
30. Ability to cognitively engage every athlete during the practices
31. Focus on decision-making development
32. Develop athlete's technical and physical skills as outlined in the "Core Skills" program, Addendum 3.
33. Plan, implement and control pre-game preparation, visualization
34. Effective use of 3 minute warm-up prior to game
35. Ability for coach to take time to teach the "technique" for individual and team
36. Coach is able to modify instruction/training on the fly

37. Coach outlines the specific duties required of the assistant coach BEFORE practice and communicates practice plan ahead of time
38. Coach stresses positives and helps teach by using a mistake as a learning opportunity
39. Coach understands feed forward to support the athletes development in a positive way
40. Coach understands the difference between winning today's game and developing young hockey players
41. Coach maintains team discipline including: time on ice, passing, penalties, and team play
42. Coach informs players of reason for missing shifts, playing less or more
43. Coach informs athletes on their position on the team depth and what athletes must do in order to climb up the depth chart.

Essential performance monitoring:

44. Individualization of training for each athlete can be specific to weakness and strength
45. Skill in analysis of psychological preparation (pre-game speech)
46. Ability to have athletes peak at the appropriate times
47. Delivery of training sessions aligned to short and long term performance goals
48. Assist the Strength and Conditioning Coordinator, or other designated personnel, to develop, implement, and monitor conditioning and skills enhancement

programs designed to improve athletic ability and performance
49. Measure physical strength and conditioning programs to give feedback to players and parents.
50. Hold a player evaluation meeting that covers players on and off-ice evaluations.

Season Plan

The main purpose of the Season Plan is to set out the expectation for the team comprised of the players and parents. It is my opinion that the Association should hand the head coach a template for a Season Plan that can be tweaked.

The Plan will alleviate a ton of future problems by communicating to players and parents what the upcoming season will entail. I like to think of it as my "sales pitch" to my customers – the players and parents.

- Training. Outline how much training the team will do. Approximately how many minutes of practice time we will benefit from over the entire season.
- Games. A quick synopsis of league and playoff play. Add anticipated start and finish dates.
- Dryland. How much dryland/ off-ice training will the team do?
- Video Sessions. How often and how long will these sessions take place?

- Goalie Training. What extra help will the goalies get? Professional help from in game analysis to practice training.
- Summer Training. Outline the expectations for Spring and Summer.
- Tournaments. Provide an outline of tournaments that are likely to be a part of the upcoming season.
- Player testing. Testing analysis on the ice and off the ice to help coaches articulate to parents strengths and weaknesses of individual players.
- Mental Toughness. Any sport psychology pieces should be added.
- Core Skills. Outline the individual and team core skills to be developed. Perhaps include the age appropriate Core Skills in Addendum 3.
- Specialized coach instruction. Any power skating, shooting, puck handling professionals should be added.
- Block Plans. A preview to the Block Plan for specific timeframes for the season.
- Coach philosophy. Discuss the coaching philosophy for the team. Meet association's philosophy.
- Team rules. Any rules out of the ordinary should be outlined.
- Important Dates. Coaches should identify holidays where hockey training will NOT form part of that weekend.

Likewise, coaches should address days where family vacations are not acceptable.
- Player Expectations. The coach will address expectations of the players, time to arrive to practice, games, video, dryland – etc.
- Leadership Training. Discuss how leadership will be a focus for each player on the team and outline how this training will happen. (Should form part of the Association's template for each age group.)
- Budget. With the exception of travelling to tournaments and games, the budget should include everything from above and bring the assessment of the season to a $. The season plan does not need to break down costs into each category – YET.
- Timeline. Player's goal setting. Player evaluations and review of goals. Player and parent feedback.

Block Plans

During my first edit, some of my readers (namely my Dad and Aunt Sandra) found this part a little difficult to understand, so I will try my best to introduce to you what the Block Planning is and how it is significant for both the coaches and players.

By way of example, I want to show you my BLOCK plan for a AAA Bantam team. For this particular year, I used 6 BLOCKS, from which I picked out the "focus for training" for each time frame.

To keep myself on track, I selected an assortment of skills from the "SKILLS CHECKLIST FOR BANTAM" (attached under Addendum 3) that I thought were appropriate for the BLOCK ONE.

Also, because I share each BLOCK ahead of time with both parents and players, I thought that in my BLOCK ONE, I would also illustrate my expectations for players and coaches. I did not do this for BLOCK 2-6. And this further gives the athletes that make my team a more in depth view of the expectations rather than the shorter player expectations addressed in the Season Plan.

EXAMPLE - BLOCK ONE – Bantam AAA

Expectations:

Block plans are a time period where certain skills will be focused on. Focus for the team will no longer be to "touch" on areas, instead have a firm plan in hand with the intention of teaching and to sink in concepts that involve both TEAM play and INDIVIDUAL play that will form the backbone of the style we would like to implement this season. Areas in each Block Plan include:

1. Timeframe for the Block
2. Team concepts to be learned
3. Individual Concepts to be learned
4. Skill Training

Coaches will work to ensure that the team has completed the "Skills Checklist for Bantam" curriculum by the end of the season.

As coaches, we will do our best to "outwork" each player. That means - attention to every detail and preparation that will not be surpassed. To that end, we expect the players to adopt the new way to get ready for practices and games. And that means to focus and understand the plan ahead of time.

The coaches job will be to ensure that players get training plans ahead of time and the player's job is to ensure that they read the plan carefully. There is no test, just an expected **willingness** to put the time in.

I look at a season as 100 practices of 60 minutes each. That is only 6,000 minutes. We want to adopt a "no minute wasted" program. Practice will start – IMMEDIATELY. Players will be expected to have stretched in conjunction with their dryland warmup prior to the start of practice.

Our goal is not only to teach the players but to address our game plan with parents as well. Everyone needs to know that we will be putting in the "maximum" effort as coaches and we hope that this will embody the parent group as well.

This year will feature "game situation" training. And that means HITTING in practice. We will hit, without the intent to hurt, but we will hit in practice just like a game. Players will consistently be put in situations that resemble a game, and teaching points will be continuously addressed.

With our "no minute wasted" program, teaching points will often come after drills on an individual basis, which will allow the practice to continue. There will certainly be times to teach the entire group at the same time, but we will try to limit these teaching moments to "team concepts" only.

Practice starts as soon as the first player gets on the ice. Don't be late.

Players will stop in front of the net on every shooting drill. They will remain at the "side" of the crease for the next shooter to bang in rebounds if possible. Play pucks OUT – which means play until a save or the puck is WAY TOO FAR AWAY to go after.

Coaches will try not to use whistles to START drills. We will provide indicators that players will learn. A whistle means STOP. And STOP means STOPPED entirely, not moving the tiniest thing.

Shooting – No player is allowed to "shoot" the puck without first attempting to move the puck. Pull and shoot, push and shoot, stop and shoot, curl and shoot, cut and shoot, fake shot shoot, slap fake and shoot. You get the idea. I have not seen a player walk into the slot and shoot a puck hard since Squirt/Atom so we will not do this any longer in our practices. Players are refrained from shooting warmup shots from the slot. Shoot from areas that happen in a game.

Water – There will be very few "water breaks" in practice. An attempt to start drills from near the water bottles on the bench will be made, so if you are in line and near the water bottles, get some water. Please make sure that your water bottles are full.

ONE LAP or Bag Skates – we will NOT be doing either of these. So the whistle may end a drill and players are expected to race into the coaches and grab a knee. DO NOT BE LAST. We will quickly move onto the next drill, and we expect that the players will just need a "reminder" of what the practice plan already identified. We will rarely need to use the BOARD to begin a drill. Instead, the "BOARD" will often be used to call in the team to "teach a fundamental or skill" at some point **during** the drill.

Drills – as mentioned drills will be more game situational. Battle temperatures should be high. Drills will not be complicated. If you do not understand the drill, start at the back of the line. No need to ask the coaches. All drills will have names. Players will learn these names and quickly know what is expected.

Talk – simply put, we will become the best on-ice talking team in the country. It begins today.

1. Timeframe

Block ONE – forms the plan for the following 9 practices which puts our team at our first game of the season on September 9th.

Shared Practices – Aug 21, 28, Sep 4

Team Full Ice Practices – Aug 22, 24, 29, 31, Sep 5 and 7

2 - Team Play Concepts

The following team concepts will form the focus for Block ONE:

- Faceoffs – we will go over the job responsibility for each player for LOST faceoffs. The focus will be on how to regain possession of the puck through a 5 player system of puck pursuit and retrievals. The idea here is to treat every faceoff this year as if we got tortured by losing the faceoff and we need this torture to stop as quickly as possible. Faceoffs will form part of our team identity. Team readiness at every drop of the puck. And most importantly, TEAM FOCUS.

- Power Play – I feel that an effective power play can be a difference maker in games and that this critical skill should be a focus in our first block. For these particular 9 practices, we will go over team breakout and zone entries. We will also teach our "set up" and expectation for each player in the power play alignment. To begin with, we will not be stressing perfect execution rather we will be stressing decision making and keeping skilled plays simple. The power play is dangerous with precision passing. So this common element skill will be stressed. Passer and receiver will be accountable for proper positioning and ability to get open and present easy passing lanes.

- Chip passes – As these athletes get older, pressure situations arise all over the ice, and we both believe that the players must learn to keep the puck moving NORTH with support in the form of chip passes. We will be focusing on the areas on the ice that lead to these passes and teach how to support and call for "chip it" passes.

- Team Passing – we will work on moving the puck from the strong side to the weak side using D to D with a winger in an excellent post position with the stick in a great acceptance position. This will form a **basic** for our team. We will do this from all areas of the ice. Added players will then begin to force the Team Passing (a group of 5) to minimize time and enhance decision-making skills.

3. Individual Concepts

The following individual concepts will be the focus of Block One:

- 1 on 1 – at U14 gone is the deke through a defensive players legs! This will not be tolerated any longer. In - is the inside-outside drive (with a change of speed) combined with a shot from the outside (if possible). If you want to deke through players, go to stick and puck. 1 on 1's out of the corner will feature the same concepts which will involve puck protection, with players trying to win a gap/space on the defenseman and accelerate towards a shot.

- 2 on 1 – we will be working on teaching the players how to get great opportunities off this rush. They will feature all kinds of 2 on 1's, not just straight up the ice. Strong and weak side variables and solutions will be explained. Stick position, player body position, shooting angles, rebound relentlessness will all be components that will lead to our team scoring more goals.

4. Skills Training

A) Forwards: Attention will be placed on how to attack a defending player

- Use teammates DRIVING NET to attack, the use of slippery passes through the defender's triangle (stick and feet)
- Using change of speed to disrupt defensive gap
- Cross and drop (Offensive ENTRY)
- Puck protection for down low 1 on 1's, use edges to get an advantage
- Give an go to create offense
- B) Defense: Attention will be placed on how to defend an attacking player
- Angle offensive player towards the boards, BEGIN TO THINK – HOW TO WIN THE PUCK?

- Gap control – move up to get yourself to move backwards with more speed, GET BEAT IN PRACTICE MORE OFTEN, INTERRUPT THE PLAY EARLY (neutral zone)
- Proper pivots (defend the inside of the ice first)
- Properly defend a 1 v 1 and 1 v 2

Lots of 1 on 1 plays in the first 2 weeks, moving to 2 on 1's. Small area "game like" drills will also cover these two offensive and defensive skill sets.

Conclusion of Block One. Block Two, emailed out by September 5.

Player Evaluation Meetings

It is extremely important to hold at minimum ONE 10-15 minute conversation with players and parents during the season. Young players have a difficult time "properly" relaying a particular message that a coach is trying to give. This meeting helps everyone involved dive into and formulate a plan for improvement in areas deemed to need greater performance either on the ice, off, or both.

The ideal time to have this meeting is before the Christmas break. Having the meeting before the holidays lets parents decide if there might be some opportunities away from the team to improve a specific skill or weakness. Think power skating or shooting clinics.

One of my favorite off-ice evaluations has always been the beep test. And I like to do this test a couple times during the season with the parents watching. As a coach, it gives conditioning feedback that can go a long way into playing some players more than others at the end of a long tournament or series of games. And the feedback happens directly in front of the parents. A win for a lot of coaches.

Besides evaluating off-ice strength and conditioning skills, coaches must also evaluate strength of character for each player. What scouts call, "the intangibles!" This is where the leadership skills are being evaluated. These form the life skills that will follow players far beyond hockey.

Lastly, coaches will go through the "player skills checklist" to provide feedback for each player and the parents. Sometimes this process can be an eye opener for parents and players and sometimes this process will just confirm a shared view. The player's skills checklist is attached as Addendum 3.

Player and Parent Feedback

Now this is an interesting concept. Player and parents both get to evaluate the coach! Different forms are used for different age groups, but in essence, players can give their own feedback. The feedback for player and parents must NOT be shared directly with the coach. Instead these feedback forms help decision-makers determine whether or not to hire the coach again for the upcoming season. These forms are usually presented to players and parents in January. Some clubs have finally gone online with feedback questionnaires!

These feedback forms which form part of Gold Standard Hockey, really help Associations through the re-hiring process of head coaches. Truth be told there is a severe implication in this process – putting your name on a review of the coach can have dire consequences. Associations should tread carefully in these waters. By not having a mandatory name on the feedback form can create other problems, so weighing of each feedback form should be adjusted to whether the player or parent signed the form.

Generally, the forms work very well and parents get to voice their opinions which very often don't get heard. One parent voicing a singular problem doesn't get much merit from a Hockey Director/GM or President of an Association. A whole team voicing the same opinion will get the attention of the Association.

Hey everyone, thank you for buying my book.

I hope you are enjoying the book so far. I am excited to get some feedback directly from my readers. I set up a Blog on my book site called: www.makehockeygreatagain.com

If you like or dislike some of the ideas presented so far, feel free to comment on the Blog. I will do my best to respond.

Another great source for learning is YouTube, so feel free to join my YouTube channel as a subscriber:
www.youtube.com/mikekennedy

Chapter 4

Winning Parents

What hockey teaches during the marathon JOURNEY

Hockey is a lifetime sport. I still look forward to every Thursday night! Hockey is the best sport in the world because we have a locker room. As a youth, it is a sanctuary away from parents, protected by coaches. As an adult, it is a room full of friends and laughter. In both worlds, it is a respite from everyday life.

When you become an adult, you cannot wait for hockey night – firstly to play, secondly to see your buddies and enjoy a cold one with them (or two). Many of us play into our 50'sand 60's competitively! I don't see many other team sports have this kind of connection. Most men's league (beer leaguers) play on a team all year long. Eventually, we all end up here, the longer it takes you to join the beer league – the further in hockey you must have gone!

We play hockey to compete and to challenge ourselves and our team. Friendships are made. Teammates are formed. Battles are won and lost. Life lessons are learned. We play to measure our improvement as a team and individual. The game of hockey is simple and complex. We play because we are inspired by the complexity. The success of executing a play as a team is one of the most rewarding feelings you can get.

We work at our job to challenge ourselves. Friendships are made. Teammates are formed. Deals are won and lost. Lessons are learned. We work to measure ourselves against our competitors, against the numbers from last quarter. Our job is simple yet complex. We work to execute a group/company decision, and we crave the feeling of success because of the execution.

In a sense, hockey very closely mimics the real world. Everyone is competing with each other. How do I master the skills needed to give my team/company a better chance at success and in turn enable myself to move up the depth chart into a first line player? Skills. People. Teamwork. Drive. Passion. Work ethic. These words apply directly to both worlds.

The journey of hockey is full of lessons. Many lessons can be learned by playing sports, but a few can only be learned through hockey, and here they are:

Accountability.

The team needs you to do your best. Is your best having a slice of pizza between games? Is your best taking it easy in practice? Accountability is enjoying the work required in training. The focus required to get better every second. And few other places have accountability like hockey. As players get older and the outcome is focused on winning, players begin to buy into the group mentality. A pack of wolves that are hungry. If we work together – we eat.

Perseverance.

If you haven't had a setback in hockey – good for you. However, most of us have many setbacks. Struggle and Emerge from Notre Dame comes to mind when I think about my own career. But players don't emerge because the feedback most often times sucks. What do I need to do to make this team? To get more playing time? To achieve my goals? In order to emerge, you must have perseverance and a belief in yourself. Train hard. Train smart. Find an advantage over your competitors. Unfortunately, you will not get a lot of quality feedback. Focus on getting better every second needs to be at the heart of a youth hockey player with big dreams.

Leadership.

Not everyone is a noticeable leader, but leadership disguises itself throughout hockey practices and games. You get punched in the head at a scrum – what does a leader do? A player pokes at your goalie? The point here is that there are opportunities everywhere in a hockey game to be a leader. Preparation. Getting yourself ready to play. Knowing the clock. The score/time left in a game should influence the decision you make with the puck. Focusing on the coach's words. Executing the game plan. I could go on and on, but I definitely feel that hockey has a significant advantage in Leadership.

So back to the journey of hockey. The journey is filled with learning skills that are applied to life outside hockey. We know that. The journey is filled with competitive games that test improvement. The journey is a long one. It begins at six and ends when the knees stop working. It begins in August every year and ends in April. It begins at 6 am. It must be accompanied with a thirst that is never satisfied.

Parents Journey

As a parent, you are part of this incredible journey. It is extremely time-consuming, managing your own job and getting your kid to hockey is extremely difficult. We do it because we see the enjoyment of our kids, the enjoyment of improvement, the enjoyment of success and we want this to translate into enjoyment for their life.

Parents play a huge role in the journey. When I played pro in Germany, I asked every teammate (Canadian, American, Swedish and German) I played with a simple question: "Did your parents PUSH you?" And by push, I mean – demanding. I.e. The car ride home was often not very fun. And the collective answers were about 50/50. I do however find that the players that were "pushed" most often are the players whose equipment is dusty in the garage at the conclusion of their hockey career. The players that were "supported" by our parents, including me, are the ones who can't wait for Thursday night and enjoy watching our kids grow in the game of hockey.

I want to ensure a couple of messages get out here. Some parents do not know that they are "pushing" their kids to develop a distaste for the game.

Here is an example of a parent I coached that I was able to swing around to "support" not "push." The game is over. The ride home is coming. The player always loathes the ride home because the same question is coming after each game. "How did you think you played?" Simple question. But, because of the frequency becomes an extremely irritating question. The player does not want to answer. The parent wants an answer. The player can only think of, "What can I say that will get my parent off my back?" Resentment sets in. Frustration climbs. WTF. "I played bad." Happy? I hate getting this question…remains the only thought.

I asked the parent how they would feel towards their boss, it their boss at the end of every day, came into your office and asked, "How did you do today?" Day one. "I did great, hit a lot of my targets, set up some important meetings and basically killed it." Day three. GFY.

So we discussed what the reason for the question was. "I just want to get his thoughts on the game." And we came up with a very different question. "What were the best parts of the hockey game?" The question immediately stopped being about the player, and now focused on the team.

Do you know what my mom asked me after most of my youth hockey games? "Stop sticking your head out the window; it is freezing in here" as we drove down the 401 and I tried to cool off!

Word to parents – what is your expectation that your son/daughter plays a great game every time? Answer – NHL players can't even do this, why should a youth player be able to play great every time? I think a realistic expectation is that your child applies effort and receives enjoyment from the game.

School Grades – report card, feedback
So you think your son is smart? He got a 90% average. A 3.5GPA. It is measured. We have a statistic to drill into. A measurement against our competitors. Problem is – different schools, teachers, subjects all factor into a grade. That is why in the US, there are two standard tests for high schoolers – SAT and ACT tests. The playing field is leveled.

So you think your son is good at hockey? He scored 30 goals. It is measured. The problem is – different teams, levels, competitors all factor into the statistic. In hockey, there is no way to measure what scoring 30 goals mean. 30 goals at AA is completely different than 30 goals at AAA. It is like the "strength of schedule in NCAA football." But what about an offensively gifted coach vs a defensive coach. If you score 30 on a defensive team that only scored 100 goals, you probably are a rock star. It is difficult to measure offensive success.

My buddy Phil Huber played on a powerhouse WHL team, the Kamloops Blazers. Hubie scored 152 points. What the heck...? Hubie you are a grinder and mucker, how the heck did you score that many points in junior? Answer: "I have been the same size I am now at 15 years old – 5'11" and 210lbs. – a MAN CHILD. I simply ran over the other kids." Hubie was a massive part of our DEL Championship team in Munich. He adjusted his skill set to be a penalty killer, clock killer, and defensive meister. Our team won the championship because we had 4 trusted lines that our coach, Sean Simpson could utilize at any moment. Hubie accepted his role and we won! Simple eh?

Report Card.

It is important for players to get feedback. To get a report card from your coach. To understand your strengths and weakness. To implement a plan to improve BOTH.

Lastly, if your son scored 10 goals or less as a forward, you are probably playing in a division too high for his skill set. It is my opinion, in order to develop skills like learning how to use time and space to create good hockey plays, players need to be in the right time factored environment which will maximize the learning curve of these skills. If the pace is too fast, my guess is that you will never learn to master the skill. Slow down. Learn it. Then speed it up. Go down a level, learn to score 30+ goals, learn how to be a valuable player, becoming a key player will only help the long-term development. It will not hurt. Sometimes I say to parents, "Wayne Gretzky scored 360 goals in one season as a youth player, do you think it hurt his development?"

Moving up

Moving up is good right? Playing with older kids. Faster kids. Better players all around you. Why not? You will have to decide for yourself if that is the best route. But here is a general rule: if you move up and are NOT on the power play, are not counted on during the most important parts of the game – then you should NOT move up. But if you continue to be an impact player, then go for it. Challenge yourself.

At some point our 16-year-olds play with 20-year-olds. Talk about an adjustment. Beards…showers…you get the idea. There's a great article about Will Butcher, a defenseman for New Jersey Devils and a product of Denver and Jim Montgomery's program. The article talks about how Will stayed at Denver for 4 years and did not pursue pro until he graduated. The article is titled, "There is no rush to development," and this is an example of how Will pursued his degree without losing his ability to play pro later.

Great, it worked for Will. But the article doesn't talk about Will's youth hockey career and the fact that he did 'rush' development because he was NOT challenged. He did move up, he had to. He needed to. Is this considered rushing development -> At 15 he was playing U18AAA, and at 16 he left home for Detroit and the NTDP program. So the article is a bit off, but there is a fact – he continued to play where he was challenged. And obviously, he played at Denver for 4 years because he felt like he was getting better and the game was still challenging him.

The key piece to rushing development to move up (whatever words you choose) is that players need to be challenged and if players need to move up to be challenged – go for it.

Moving out

Many players can't wait to leave home and "go for it" with a program that has a home for them. And many parents support this route. Prep schools. Junior programs. And now even U16 and U18 programs all provide the billeting experience. My advice to parents is relatively simple – if your kids are begging you to go, get ready to watch their games on the internet. But if your kid is only lukewarm to the idea, then finding a good coach and team locally won't necessarily drag down their chances for the long term. It can happen, but it is unlikely. By the time most kids graduate high school, they are READY to leave home, and junior programs are a plenty looking for $ to keep their program going.

Junior

At 17, most players have matured into their bodies and minds. Not totally, but partially. Most kids understand the amount of training their competitors are doing. If training becomes burdensome, then players will soon be stars in their beer leagues at home. However, if training becomes the highlight of each day, players will have doors open, and opportunities abound.

The average age of a college NCAA Scholarship for freshman that are playing is 20.4 years old. So the training a player does from 17-20 is critical to success during college. Find a great program with a great coach/teacher that understands the offensive part of the game. Hone your skills. Speed them up. And find ways to awe scouts/recruiters.

Support System

This is a tough part to delicately present. The reason that it is so tough is that most parents that think they are being supportive – AREN'T. More than 50% of parents are in the category of – not knowing that they are NOT supportive.

I think it might be best to begin by going into further detail about what constitutes unsupportive, negative influence on a player:

- Over-involvement – taking excessive interest in the sport, attempting to coach your child (sometimes from the stands), communicating with them during a game (sign language must stop)
- Unrealistic expectations – focused on outcomes, expecting the 6th place team to beat the 1st place team, hoping yes, expecting – no

- Adding pressure – becoming nervous, having parental anxiety, (there is enough pressure on the kids to perform, parents don't need to feel any pressure)
- Excessive criticism following a game – wouldn't this be nice if excessive criticism were employed after a practice instead?
- Negative display – angry, verbal, nonverbal, physical (Ever bang on the glass to get your son's attention? Ever shake your head in disapproval?)
- Criticism of the referee
- Criticism of the coach
- Crazy cheering

Parents will at some point hear that a teammate on the team is getting burned out. What they NEVER hear is that the player is their own child. What thoughts come to mind? Not enough ice time. Too much pressure. Not enough passion. Maybe. But do you want to know the most likely reason kids quit – overinvolved parents! It reduces the enjoyment and increases anxiety. And over-involvement is a significant contributor to youth players dropping out of competitive sports. And most parents do not even know that they exhibit many of the behaviors listed above.

Positive Support System

In competitive sports like hockey, we as parents often find ourselves playing the sport from the stands. Finding ourselves in the moment. Being able to share in the training and outcomes. I find this trait to be most common from parents that didn't play the sport or parent's that weren't athletes growing up. (It is their turn to compete through their kids). It is important to recognize that the game of hockey is for your child, not you. And that the training and competitions are for the athletes, not the parents.

I encourage all parents to learn to watch the TEAM and not to focus only on your son or daughter. You will find the game more exciting, and you will begin to see the game through the eyes of your child because you can't really watch yourself play (live). Another tip is to sometimes stand at ice-level and see how difficult it is to read the plays. From up top, the game is slow and easy to interpret, but from the glass, the bench or the ice – it is FAST and difficult which is partly what makes it so fun.

A positive supporting parent can be critical of the effort. The effort is the backbone of sport and beyond. It is sometimes shocking when it is missing. Look for hints and clues that could result in a lackluster effort. Was it diet, sleep, stress, anxiety, or something else. And if you can begin to identify it, put a plan in place to eradicate it. Get help if you need to.

My son, a U16AA goalie, had an awful game at a semi-final tournament, a six-hour drive from home. I took 30 minutes in the car before I opened up the conversation with him. It took me 30 minutes because I was weighing whether to say anything at all. Sometimes it is better just to forget a bad performance. But many times the lack of saying something can be a lot worse. So I prepared a plan for what I wanted to get out of the conversation.

And what I wanted was reflection. Can you reflect on what happened <u>prior</u> to the game? The timeline leading up to it was going to be the TOPIC of the conversation. What do you know, he told me that everything was great, he felt great, strong, flexible, confident and ready. Shoot. What now? At least he was prepared and ready. So I moved to ask him what I can do to help him? What type of training adjustments need to be made to improve his success? At 16 you are lucky to get any answer, but the answer I got was, "I need to improve my breakaways." Better than nothing and we left it at that, and I alerted the Head Coach of this conversation.

We all want to be involved; I get that. But you need to have REAL conversations with your kids. Ask them what bothers them. Let them be critical of <u>YOU</u>. 99% of the age group competitors in hockey will be beer leaguers really soon – and if you are not ok with that, then you should lace up the skates yourself and go play for your son or daughter.

Parents tend to get a little analytical in their hockey quest. Goals, assists, ice time all form areas of analysis. Questioning the coach. Critical of decisions made. Lines assembled. The list goes on. And to that I say, for every time you want an answer about a coaching decision – please go into your child's classroom first and start asking teachers about homework and test scores. Because trust me, 99% of the beer leaguers will be far better off with better report cards than worrying about a coaching decision in a youth hockey game.

Do you know what almost every kid wants from their parent: just sit there and watch. That is it. That is the most supportive we can be. Tough isn't it?

> Billy Mills, 1964 Olympic Gold Medalist – "The ultimate is not to win, but to reach within the depths of your capabilities and to compete against yourself to the greatest extent possible. When you do that, you have dignity. You have the pride. You can walk about with character."

"Our desire to better ourselves and develop our natural gifts is what makes us all distinctly human. We all want to be successful in our most important competitive pursuits. All of us want to test our talents against others' talents and remain dedicated to our highest achievement. All of us want to perform at our best by competing against our own standard of excellence. Indeed, many of us want to prove that our best is better than the rest." Jim Afremow, *Champions Mind*

> "The perfect performance is the one which, when the whistle blows or you finish the workout, you can honestly say that you gave your absolute best, regardless of the outcome. You will either win or learn something that will make you stronger for the next effort." Jim Afremow, Champions Mind

Apolo Ohno, Olympic Gold Medalist – "Winning does not always mean coming in first. Second. Or third. Even fourth – they are wins too, no matter what anyone says. Real victory is in arriving at the finish line with no regrets."

You control your attitude and effort every day. Do your best by discovering new borders and extending physical limits. Put the process first. Achieve daily acts of excellence.

> "Look for patterns in your mental and physical pregame tendencies to transform any poor patterns into top-notch patterns."- Jim Afremow, Champions Mind.

Becoming GREAT is a CHOICE!

Chapter 5

Players – MAZIMIZE YOUR POTENTIAL

Love the game first.

Our parents put us in hockey. In Canada and the Northern USA, this is a natural explanation – because most everyone else is put in hockey. In other places, my guess is that the parent has a connection to the sport and sees a value in hockey. Some parents have played, others have not and get into the sport because their friend recommends the sport. Some kids get into hockey because they liked to skate at a birthday party they went to. However you get into the sport does not matter - the fact you are now playing is a celebration!

All sports at their core are designed to be fun to play. And, at the end of the day, every match is fun when the match is competitive for both teams. Players are striving to put in place valuable information designed by coaches to give a competitive advantage. Fun – want the definition? -> Something that provides amusement or enjoyment. I am confident that "fun" is interpreted in many different fashions when it comes to sports.

When we are very young (5-8years old), we are often put on a team consisting of 13-15 players and a coach with a son/daughter on the team. Instantly we have been put into a group with 13-15 different opinions on what a hockey season should look like and most times, we have 13-15 different definitions of "fun," and many of these definitions are linked to parents that don't understand what "fun" is and how it applies to hockey.

Success breeds passion.

I want to move forward towards helping parents and players adopt a "love" for the game. The "love" begins with SUCCESS. Simply put – scoring goals will drastically improve the desire to learn more. I am pretty sure that this applies outside sports – if you are really good at math, my bet is you "love" math.

So essentially, if we want our young players to love hockey, it makes a lot of sense to have enough success to begin to fall in love with the sport. Litle success equals -> maybe this sport is not for me.

Friendships first.

For a youth hockey player, parents can make a significant impact on how fun the sport "stays." Notice I did not say "becomes?" Parents have to learn one thing that will make them an excellent hockey/sports parent – it is not for you, it is for the kids. Moreover, when parents can watch their kids play hockey without ever looking at the scoreboard to see which team had more success on a particular day, then we have a parent who supports their player and supports the coaches and understands that the score represents VERY LITTLE about the game of hockey. There is a lot more going on than just a scoreboard.

THREE stages of a youth hockey player's career

Stage 1 - Pre-Puberty – Keep the Love going

Up until kids begin the puberty phase we need to remember that the most important thing we can get from hockey is – WE WANT the kids to WANT TO GO TO THE RINK for Practices and Games. The desire to want to go. Without this desire, we are going for "other" reasons. Want me to name the most significant reason youth players go when they don't want to? Answer: Our parents make us go.

Think about that for a second. How as parents can we avoid "making our kids go?" Easy answer – stop being so critical of performance.

All kids need somebody in "their" corner. Why not their own parents? Yes it is extremely tough to deal with your kid not excelling or even worse – giving a lack of effort, but we must remind ourselves that kids have ups and downs and to be quite frank, there are many athletes in the NHL who have good games, bad games, games with incredible work ethic and average work ethic.

Perhaps instead of parents being so critical we can stand back a little and examine "why did my kid play so poorly or why did my kid play so well?" The answers might amaze you. Here are some answers that get missed.

Played well: ate the right amount of the right food at the right time. Slept well the night before. Had a great day at school (maybe did well on a test). Coaches said the right words to make the player feel good. These are just a common few.

Played awful: ate too much, ate at the wrong time, feel bloated. Slept poorly. Had an awful day at school, stressed out about a test or report card that is coming. Coaches make the player feel less valuable and perhaps singled out the player.

Any of these can severely negatively impact performance. Moreover, my bet is that most parents have never noticed any of these indicators. So the real question becomes – how can I communicate with my kid so that I am aware of all the things in his/her life that may influence their performance?

Stage 2 – Puberty – Timing of this has implications

This is a tough time for anybody let alone athletes that are soon getting naked in front of each other. Puberty would be a breeze if everyone got it at exactly the same time. How much easier would it be for an entire team of 14-year-olds hitting puberty at the same time? Growth spurts. Awkward performance. Zits.

Showers. Moreover, the desire to play the game changes at this time as well.

However, puberty does not hit at the same time, the average range is from 13-16, and that becomes problematic for late bloomers. Their size is late in coming, their strength is late in coming, and their (testosterone for boys) is late in coming which affects aggressiveness on the ice.

To remember this important point: If my son hits puberty early (likely he will be stronger and more aggressive) you as a parent should understand that your player is lucky to be ahead of the pack, but the pack is…coming. And if you are late getting to puberty (like I was), then you need to know that you WILL grow and that if you can keep up with the pack, then when it finally hits you, it will give you a significant boost. Hockey is incredible because there are spots for every kind of player: skillful, fast, strong, big, quick, creative, and a most unusual characteristic – understands the game better, known as "hockey sense."

Stage 3 - Post-puberty

Once we get the group to this period of time, we are now all back on equal footing, and the intensity is jacked up to the max. I read once that aggressiveness in a person is actually a habit to show off to a woman (girls) to prove your mightiness. This may be true, but for me, it was only one thought – how do I get the puck from this monster? Don't back down.

What are the best ways to get better?

Stay Coachable

No matter how experienced you become, remain coachable. Learn everything – learn: Why? How? When? Understand that hockey is chaos on the ice and that the chaos is broken down into scenes of familiarity. With the familiarity comes calm and with calm comes execution.

Be a Student of the game

"Always stay coachable. For growth, we must be willing to leave out what we already know so we can be open to learning from others with special skills, particularly our coaches and teammates. Even the best athletes, those at the very top of their game, continually seek to learn new techniques and hone their skills. Be a good listener and accept corrections and act on them." Jim Afremow, Champion Mindset.

Focus.

Players must learn to focus on the coach. Pay attention to the demonstration. Copy the move. Repeat. Fail. Repeat. Endless desire to get it right. Players that move quickly through skills training can adequately adjust their body to achieve the required skill. These adjustments are best developed by becoming a better athlete (playing multiple sports or training hard in off-ice programs) and learning body awareness activated by (a,b,c) agility, with balance and co-ordination inserted. Play all sports –

simple. Every time you kick a soccer ball, swing a bat – you just got better at hockey!

If you have designs on your son playing collegiate hockey, there are a couple of realities that must come to the forefront.

1. Developing a hunger for improvement
2. Enjoying the failure on the way to success (if you aren't falling down enough, you are not trying hard enough!)

So, what about the fun? I think that competitive people should refrain from using the word "fun" and replace it with "challenge." This is more appropriate to how we want to shape the environment to lead to success. Any challenge for a competitive athlete is FUN. Keep the environment challenging!

Learn to Visualize

Build a sharp and distinct mental image of your ideal performance state. Your body takes all graphic mental images as if they are real and happening at the present time. As you visualize the ideal performance state, you are actually creating it. Visualization works best when your mind is clear, and your body is at ease. Regulate the breathing tempo with full inhale, full exhale. This will help you get in the proper state for visualization and you can concentrate on the images of execution.

The visualization movements must be applied to a game situation. Moreover, the skill must be completed without "thinking" of executing the skill; rather, by assembling the information coming at you. Using chunking, the ability to recognize this pattern, the player performs the skill without even really realizing all the information that has been processed. Execution. It just happens...

Start a Performance Routine

I think most of us know that pro hockey players have routines. Some are quirky, and some are downright crazy. Carter Hart, goaltender for Team Canada at the World Juniors 2017/18 had to leave the ice last to feel like he was in control of his surroundings.

A good routine sets our mind at ease. It allows us to mentally get in the zone as we prepare to play. It is comfortable. It is automatic.

The question is – when do we start to develop a routine? The answer is – the sooner, the better. In youth hockey, often the warmup is limited to 3 minutes, but there are still a ton of opportunities for routines to take place.

Pre-game preparation: where you sit, how you put your equipment on, what you think about, what you say, how alert you become, the butterflies, when you take the ice, what you do when you take the ice, how you handle the puck, how you warm up your feet, how you shoot – the list goes on and on. Moreover, young players need to learn to begin this routine as early as possible. Sticking to your routine from one game to the next will help reduce weaker games and put players into a mindset that every game is capable of your best performance.

Some keys to help young players develop a top-notch performance routine:

1. Visualize the plays that make you a great player
2. Keep a list of the keys that make you play your best. A list might look like this:
   - F - Skate hard all game, every shift
   - F/D - Be first to loose pucks
   - F - Involve the defense in the offensive zone
   - F/D - Be focused and ready on faceoffs
   - F - Find scoring areas away from the puck
   - D - Close the gap with better speed following offensive rushes
   - D – Join the rush when the opportunity is there
   - G – play all dumped pucks
   - G – be aggressive when player is being cut off
   - G – stay in the routine, when good or bad things happen
3. Breathing. Deep, full breaths push the mind into performance mode.
4. Body Language. Act like a champion. To be really good, you have to be brimming with confidence and exude some swagger.
5. Intensity. 15 minutes before a hockey game, the laughter subsides, and the business of the task at hand comes to the forefront. Build the intensity.

Routines change over time. As we get older and wiser, we see the signs that ever so minimally help our performance, and we lace these changes into our routine. A good sign is noticing that your routine has changed slightly without ever even thinking about it. Finely tuned over a number of years!

Feel your Body Awareness

Are you able to listen to your body and mind? Can you feel your body? Elite athletes are in tune with their body, and the awareness of how they feel is paramount. Elite athletes can feel:

- Muscle soreness and strength
- Fatigue – mentally and physically
- Energetic – mentally and physically
- Tightness and flexibility
- Diet – athletes can feel what food makes them play best and when to eat it

What is essential for an athlete is to go over the timeline leading up to how you feel! So, if you feel amazing and energized before a game – what routine leading up to this point led to this feeling? How can we replicate it? If your body or mind feels less than the expectation – why? What happened? And how do you set a plan around not letting this happen again?

- Diet
- Sleep
- School – exams, tests, homework, anxiety
- Personal life – girlfriend, boyfriend, parents, travel

The list goes on, but the idea here is to start to put a routine in place that maximizes YOUR performance. Listen to your body and mind. Listen to the timeline leading up to great performances. Repeat it. Tweak it. Moreover, enjoy the game of "fine tuning" your pre-game preparations.

Mental Toughness

There are tons of books on this subject, and for those that struggle with this, I suggest diving deeper into the subject. For me though, mental toughness is the ability to perform without the added anxiety of what the game represents. Gold medal game – is this another hockey game? Alternatively, should I prepare differently? Should I take this game more seriously? Should I focus more? The answers are: if I need to do anything differently, then my routine is wrong. Do what you do for your success. Trust your preparation routine. Control what is in your control. The outcome will definitely happen. You can't control the outcome every time, but you can control your own performance.

Mental Toughness means that athletes refrain from:
- Stressing out about a big game (too excited or overly worried)
- Trying too hard, overeager, tense, reckless
- Getting over-emotional because of the magnitude of the game

Mental Toughness means that athletes focus on:
- Play hard every shift

- Intangibles – discipline, stick to the game plan and remain calm
- Trust – your training, your preparation and your strategy
- If I play hard, the score will take care of itself

The BIG game.

I am a believer that when the BIG game arrives, the job of the coach is to remind his athletes that they are well prepared and that their only job is to go out and play. If players can summon the enjoyment of the game to the forefront, my bet is they will have a great game. Big games are what all players WANT. However, many fail to have the best performance because of the anxiety. Anxiety needs to be stomped on, and coaches, teammates, and parents can definitely help players that struggle with this emotion. Fear of failure must be stripped from an athlete's mindset and replaced with the enjoyment of the challenge.

When many young players play their best hockey, it is because they feel no pressure. OK. So in a pressurized environment, like a gold medal game, coaches need to let the steam out of the pot by sending the team a simple message – "I believe in you." Isn't that all that is needed. You got to the big game, keep it up is all that is needed.

RELISH your Role

There is a fine line between accepting your role in a game and the way you play in practice.

For every hockey team, there are simply not enough minutes in a hockey game for every player to be a scorer. If you get put into a "defensive role" on a team, it is most likely that you were put there because others on the team were assigned to an offensive role. These roles can change, but until they do, the best way to get an increased bump up in the hierarchy of a team is to do what the coach wants from you. Moreover, the only way a player can do that is to ENJOY the role of being a "role" player. That is why we call it "role." Being a role player is a critical role!

When you enjoy it and you practice hard, an opportunity will come forward. Lines change. Player's get injured. Be ready for your chance. Practice hard and stay ready for an increased position on the team. Until it happens, don't moan or mope or be a drag on the team. Be the best you can be at being a role player – your chances of moving up the depth chart will go way up. It may be the next year and if it is -> spend as much time as you can on enhancing your skills so that when the team forms again the following season, you are ready for a move up and ready for the pressure to make tons of skill plays.

Once you take your role and relish it – success will follow. Take it with pride and enjoy being a "defensive defenseman" or a "penalty killer" or a "clock killer." A clock killer is a dependable forward who understands that scoring is not expected from him or his line.

What is expected of a role player? For a great role player who has excellent GAME HABITS, he must be able to:
- To be reliable defensively.
- To play hard all around the ice.
- To play the body every time, never swinging away from a possibility to hit someone.
- To forecheck ruthlessly.
- To block shots fearlessly.
- To backcheck relentlessly.
- To turnover the puck rarely.
- To get pucks out of the defensive zone.
- To get pucks deep into the offensive zone.

These are the markings of a great "role" player. These players are the unsung heroes. The soul of a team. The heartbeat. These are the players that never give up – even when the score is 5-0. They have only 1 gear – full throttle. Yes, they may be lacking in offensive skills, but they make up for it in effort. And teams can ride the energy of a role player and a role line.

Many parents have no idea that the "role style" player is such a rewarding position. As players get older and this position becomes a bigger part of "team success" coaches often point out the role players and ask the rest of the team to play "more like these guys" who pour their blood, sweat, and tears out for the team. The role players will gladly choose to WIN the game over losing the game and scoring a goal. These players may not get the same ice time as the skill players, but you get the skill player's admiration. Moreover, coaches love these players. I don't expect all parents to understand this, but I do expect that players begin to understand this and learn to relish this role as they go through their youth hockey journey.

For parents that have problems with the fact that your son/ daughter may be getting less powerplay time and less time in general on the ice, I want to point out that you signed up for rep/travel hockey and you accepted that some years you would get more ice time and other years less ice time. I hope that over the course of a minor hockey career that the minutes equal out to a negligible point. If they don't perhaps your son/daughter has been playing consistently at a level too high for their ability. Consider moving down a level to get the minutes of a skill player.

To further this thought, I want to zoom in on the 2014 Sochi Olympics where team USA and Canada were favorites to meet in the Gold medal game. It didn't happen, but we can still look back and see how each team positioned their lines as "skilled players" and "role players." What is so cool about the Olympics is that you have mega-millionaires that get assigned to a "role" player duty. A demotion. They don't look at the coach and say, "why aren't I a skill guy, I run the powerplay on my team, and I got 85 points in the NHL last year." What they say is, "ok, sure, I can do that." Even though they may not have blocked shots or thrown body checks for a long time, they know what is expected of them, and they shove all their cards in the middle and say to the coaches and their teammates, "I'm all in, I will do whatever you need."

Let's examine the 2014 Olympics. There are 6 players listed from Team Canada's / USA rosters who accepted a "role change," and relished helping their team in any way possible.

<u>Canada – 17 goals scored – 3 against</u>
John Tavares - 42:38 – ZERO points
Matt Duchene – 43:00 – ZERO points
Rick Nash – 60:32 – 1 assist
<u>USA – 20 goals scored – 12 against</u> (lost bronze medal 5-0)
Max Pacioretty – 51:43 - 1 assist
Blake Wheeler – 29:26 - 1 assist
Ryan Callahan – 85:22 - 1 assist

My point here is that had any of these players been given the "you are our guy" and played in the 90-minute range as the top scorers played, they would have all fared much better in offensive production.

Also, this is a shout out to all Jr. College and Pro coaches, if these elite, best in the world players can't put up points without significant ice time, how can your plumber/mucker 3rd and 4th line guys do it? Answer – they can't. So when John Tavares takes his role seriously, he changes his game – to a safer, right side of the puck strategy (right side of the puck is a strategy -> mostly employed by role players that when calculating the probability of the puck bounce either offensively or defensively, the "role" player always cheats to the defensive side of puck battles. Offensive players (skill players) often cheat to the offensive side of the puck battle and hope that the puck will bounce their way. A role player never does this.

How did Johnny T (Tavares) end up +3 with no points? He understood that production from him wasn't what the team was looking for, the team was chasing a gold medal, and when you got a player as impressive as Tavares changing his game for the betterment of the team, your chance of success just skyrocketed.

Relish your ROLE in GAMES not practices.

To conclude the "relish your role" section, I want to remind coaches that players who don't possess the necessary skills of the top scoring lines, should NOT be working on "role" game habits in practice. What I mean is that these players are the group that NEEDs more skillful practice opportunities to improve. Practice means to practice the tougher skilled plays. Remember this -> It is ok to have the 3rd line play a "relish your role" style in a game, but please let these players work on their abilities to make skilled plays all over the ice in practice. No dumps. No off the glass plays.

So the long winded point here is simple – you can teach safe hockey way more easily than you can teach offense. Use practice to keep working on your skilled plays – the plays that make the people/scouts watching want to know which number was that guy or gal? Always be ready for your chance to move from role to skilled!

Preparation

"Take personal responsibility for all areas of your preparation and performance. You are responsible for maintaining a great attitude, expending your best effort during practice and in competition, and showing character on and off the playing field." By Jim Afrremo, Champions Mind

Build confidence through preparation. Nothing can take away that feeling deep inside of pride and satisfaction that I was utterly prepared to perform my best.

Preparation is a separator. It provides confidence. It invokes belief. Moreover, most youth athletes have no idea how to prepare for a game.

Seriously, if you want to play your best, your mindset needs to be dialed in at least 30 minutes before the game. The joking slowly subsides and the approach to game time is filled with anticipation, the calm before the storm. The game is filled with one on one battles and many times the player that is the most ready to compete wins the majority of the battles. Compete. A word that is critical to success but backed up with preparation. The mind must be ready. How do I get there?

My saying is to "act like a pro." But how?

Excellent Preparation Timeline

Here is a timeline of a U16AAA <u>team that knows how to prepare</u> for a hockey game.

7:00 pm – Game time

5:45 pm – arrive at the rink

5:50 pm – unpack all gear and hang up, put bags under benches, change into warm-up gear, greet players, lots of chatting going on

6:00 pm – head out to prepare yourself for the game, 15 minutes of team two-touch - soccer, laughter, joking, being together as a team

6:15 pm – soccer has finished, and each player completes their own 10-15 minutes dynamic movements routine followed by 5 minutes of stretching. Time to visualize the game, strategy to employ, individual preparation is encouraged.

6:35 pm – back to locker room. Music if any has faded to silence. Players speak intimately about the task at hand. <u>The upcoming game is the only topic of conversation.</u>

6:50 pm – fully ready, waiting for last-minute remarks from the coach, energy boiling, the focus is entirely dialed in on the coach and the jobs the players must do to be successful

This is not an easy task for a group of young hockey players. It seems like it should be fairly straight forward, but in reality this is how most teams prepare for a hockey game:

7:00 pm – Game time

5:45 pm – arrival

5:50 pm – some players hang gear, some have their bags turned sideways, sticks are a mess, water bottles are not filled, but music is turned up loud

6:00 pm – team warmup. Laughing joking continues throughout. Only a couple players break away from the group to do a serious dynamic warmup. Soccer continues to 6:30 pm. Laughing and stories about anything but hockey are the main topics.

6:30 pm – music blasting to 6:45 pm, the room is a mess, players that want to focus can't, disruptive players control the locker room, nobody has spoken about the game or strategy.

6:50 pm – music goes off, players scramble to get ready, the coach is irritated that the team does not look ready. Coach gives a message about the points of emphasis for the game, and many blank stares look back at him.

7:00 pm – the team thinks it is ready to win the hockey game. Nothing could be further from the truth.

A true professional is always trying to improve and does not care whether or not somebody is watching.

Give it ALL you got

Keep focused on the present. Don't lose track of your primary goal – get better every second. Improvement comes from focusing your energy on what is in front of you, not next week, next year. Mastering a skill takes time, and the ability to recover the skill in the blink of an eye with perfect execution takes even longer.

Let go of trying to control your skills – merely allow them to happen by reading and reacting on the ice. Once your body can execute without thinking, it is a magnificent moment. Enjoy the process; the results will come.

To get better value from your training there needs to be a piece of the training that is entirely random. Where the puzzle does not always fit together normally. I think we all realize that no two scenarios are exactly the same. There are, however, thousands of scenarios that are SIMILAR. A 2 on 1 is a good example. The defense can react in many different ways, but it is important in our training to insert unorthodox ways to defend the offensive player.

Two good things can come out of having the defensive player try unusual defending techniques. First, the offensive player will learn how to keep his head up and watch closely for signs of unusual activity. (The defenseman might bull rush the player with the puck, or slide right at him or…) Over time, the offensive player with the puck will figure out solutions to the unpredictable behavior. Secondly, the defenseman will learn how to perfect techniques like sliding at the puck carrier, or going to one knee as Doughty does, enhancing his ability to break plays up and quite frankly, enhancing his ability to break the play up and begin the attack. Other moves like faking to attack the puck carrier and pulling back need hours and hours of training.

The underlying theme here is – if you are coaching your defenseman to "just take away the pass," then you are old school, and the defender is not learning as much as they could be.

What do Scouts look for?

News, just out: ALL Scouts, whether Junior, College or Pro DO NOT CARE much about defensive hockey.

Reality: The belief has always been the same, and it is still the same today – Which players stand out in a hockey game?

Offensive players stand out! A defenseman that moves the puck with their head up and can join the rush for the attack stands out! A defenseman that has poise with the puck under pressure stands out! Any defenseman can wrap the puck around the boards which I usually call "giving your problem to the winger to solve."

Forwards that make creative plays in tiny spaces stand out. Fakes, dekes, finding the time and creating space stand out. Quick release with your head up stands out. Protecting the puck and exploding with strong edges stands out.

I have yet to see a midget defenseman get drafted to the CHL because he was good defensively, same goes for a forward. Every player that makes it to the "NEXT Level" was an offensive minded and skilled player.

The point here is that if you want to move on to the next level you have to learn how to be an impact player in the game.

Understand what IMPACT plays are. Here are some IMPACT plays:

- Skillful pass
- Great fake
- Quick release
- Countless patience
- Take a hit to make a play
- Move the puck quickly and effectively
- Effectively use your teammates
- The thirst to join attacks, be involved
- Great puck protection
- Great poise with the puck (comes with head up)
- Great puckhandling skills
- Great vision
- Great reads (interpretation)
- Explosive skating
- Great intensity
- Great escape moves

When you get to a combine event or a selection camp, goals and assists DO NOT MATTER. Making the IMPACT plays on this list over and over again – COUNT!

Hold yourself to your own Gold Standard.

Self-determination sets athletes apart.

Use goal setting to vault yourself past your competitors.

Chapter 6

Champion Goal Setting

Excellence is NOT random

Excellence is designed and achieved by setting and tenaciously pursuing ambitious goals. A long range goal mixed with a complete daily devotion. Are you in or are you out? Most young hockey players do not even realize...they are out. The question here is: are you IN OR OUT? Do you have what it takes for commitment which is really borderline – obsession. Better yet: Sustained Obsession.

How can you push yourself to the necessary levels of pain without your competitors surrounding you? It becomes infinitely easier to train hard when the player you are training with has the job you want. It gets infinitely harder to train with players that are weaker than yourself. Think about it. If you are the best in your town and you know it, it is unlikely that you will be able to push yourself hard enough to be the best in the state. Try to train with players better than you and players that have more desire than you. Can you train smarter and harder than your competitors by focusing, executing and caring about the little, tiny details in the move/skill?

The higher your goals, the more you will need to emphasize doing the right things to achieve those goals. A genuine determination to endlessly improve in all areas of your game.

> Dan Gable, hall of fame wrestler and coach: "When you finally decide how successful you really want to be, you've got to set priorities. In 25 years has a head coach, I never missed one practice. Why? Because practice is my top priority."

Jerry Rice, hall of fame NFL receiver: "*Today I will do what others won't, so tomorrow I can accomplish what others can't.*" This is how he did it: off-season training routine enabled Jerry to dominate the competition and stave off competitors. His workouts included sprinting 2.5 miles up steep hills. "Multitudes of NFL receivers came to train with him over the course of his career; nobody came back for a second off-season of training." Jim Afremow, Champions Mind.

When I think of a young athlete that dreams of playing hockey on a big stage: Junior, College or Pro, I think of the best enablers that help to make this happen. In short order, they are the BIG THREE: parents, coaches and the athlete. That is it. There will be nobody else that will help you. Yes, there will be strength trainers, dieticians, agents, advisors, you name it, there are probably a ton of other providers that will help you, but those will be extremely minimal compared to the big THREE.

Parent's role

The role of a great hockey parent is to enjoy the pursuit of developing. The best hockey parent will never look at a scoreboard to assess a game; instead, the parent will look for the seeds of new skills being applied in a game environment. Parents that watch practices should be impressed by seeing a practice habit being applied in a hockey game. Habits are created in practice and take time to apply in a game.

A great hockey parent will take a long-term approach with the only vision to keep the sport enjoyable and to keep listening to your young player. If they want "more" see if it is possible. Some young players just can't get enough – obsession is just beginning.

Goal Setting sets out a PURPOSE for you. Moreover, it sets a course to drive home results. Why am I here? What do I want to accomplish? Where do I want to play next year? How can I start to make my goals attainable? SAT's. Education. Dedication to improvement.

Short-Term Goals

The idea here is to set realistic objectives. Daily goals. Reflect on your weakness and strengths and put a plan together to improve. Complete the self-assessment of Individual Player Skills (checklist is added in ADDENDUM 4) and then draw up some short-term goals to address areas for improvement.

Medium Term Goals

The idea here is to use the short-term goals to get you to where you want to go…a) the end of this season and b) next season. This goal sets out where you want to be. A vision of your future self. See yourself. And go get it.

Team Goals

How can I make the team better? What can I personally do to help the team achieve its goals? What player can I identify with from the NHL and try to emulate?

<u>Priority</u>

Hockey goals are not the only goals that can be addressed here. Education is closely tied to hockey as players look to embark on paths that may lead to playing hockey at University. What are the goals of education?

Why is this important? Goals are a crucial mental training technique that, when the process is done properly, provide motivation, focus, confidence, the ability to overcome setbacks and the will to work hard day in and day out.

Goal Setting: It's All in the Process

The most valuable aspect of setting realistic targets, "is that it provides the coach with a simple tool for aligning your coaching purpose, core values and everyday coaching actions." Wade Gilbert.

Before setting goals/targets – it is important for the players and paerents to buy into the VISION. Is winning the league championship the goal? Or could the challenge be, "what could we achieve if we put our hearts and minds to it?" Jeff Janssen.

So the outcome – to win a league championship must have a strong foundation of principles. The principle above is putting our hearts and souls into it. What does that really mean?

Coaches need to dig into these principles and have players identify the characteristics that they actively set for themselves. Coaches only facilitate the accountability to the foundational characteristics that the players identified which will guide the team towards it's target.

Rather than walk you through goal setting by myself, I have attached a great article written by Enio Sacilotto on October 12, 2016. It is extremely well written and I adopt every single part of this goal setting process. It is important to set realistic targets that fit the desired outcome. Target is a great word because of the ability to visualize hitting it, here is what Enio writes:

"There is an enormous amount of scientific proof that athletes who set goals achieve more throughout their careers. Setting goals will help you determine where you currently are and create a plan to get you where you want to be. Goals allow you to decide on an outcome, make a plan, continually check your progress, and make the appropriate adjustments to keep you on course. A clear illustration of the process of goal setting is using a GPS (or Google Maps) to help you find a location. You input your destination into your GPS, as you begin to drive it keeps you on course, but when you take a wrong turn, the GPS will recalculate your route and set you back on the right course to reach your destination. Goal setting does the same thing. As long as you know your desired destination you can keep recalculating to ensure you reach it."

To accomplish this you have to be aware of the three types of goals you need to set; Process Goals, Performance Goals and Outcome Goals:

Process Goals

Of the three types of goals, your process goals are the most important. In hockey, they are strategically focused on the skills, techniques, strategies, and behaviors (mental training) that will help you reach your performance and outcome goals. This is taking the time to choose skills (whether mental or physical) that you would like to see an improvement in, devise a plan that will allow you to work on that area and a schedule to find time to work on these skills. This is the 'hard work' part of goal setting. This is when you get down and dirty by taking 100 draws a day, working on your footwork, trying to increase your speed or working on whatever skill you are trying to perfect.

Performance goals and outcome goals allow you to measure your work in this area and see the final results of your hard work. This is the area when the rubber hits the road. This is why your focus and energy must go into this area. You will create the habits that will raise the level of your game. By setting your process goals, your self-confidence will increase, your anxiety will decrease, your concentration will improve and you will approach the daily grind with enthusiasm. It has been proven time and time again that your individual performance will improve quicker if you focus on the process rather than the performance and outcome.

Performance Goals

Performance goals are what set the standard for what you are trying to achieve. These can be statistically based and measured. They can be used to monitor your achievement. When you have a series of measurements related to a certain part of your performance, you can go back and compare your numbers to previous results. Make sure that your performance goals are realistic, challenging and appropriate to your outcome goals. These types of goals are semi-controllable and are not solely based on outcomes. You may not win the game, but the fact that you performed well can give you satisfaction. Performance goals are the building blocks to achieve your outcome goals.

Outcome Goals

Traditionally the goals you set will look at a final outcome. For example, you may want to make a certain team, lead the team in scoring and the ultimate goal of winning a championship. All of these objectives are based on an end result. These are called outcome goals. Setting outcome goals is crucial, but you also have to know how to get to that point. When you reach an elite level in sport; skill, desire, and effort need to be focused. If this is done properly in the process and performance goal stages, then your chance of success at the outcome goal stage is much higher. Outcome goals create the big picture and are necessary for you to set. They will give you focus during the other stages.

PROCCESS	PERFORMANCE	OUTCOME
• Do quick feet agility drills everyday after practice.	• Win 100% of 50/50 loose pucks.	• Be the best defensive forward in the league.
• Work in the gym three times per week on strengthening my legs.	• Be in on the forecheck as soon as the puck is dumped in.	
• Work on angling drills everyday at practise.	• Be on my man within two seconds of him getting the puck.	
• Watch NHL video and study my shifts after every game.		

Reaching your goals is a difficult task. It requires you to be responsible and committed to doing the things necessary to reach your goal over the long term.

Set goals in all areas of your game (mental, physical, technical & tactical) and your life (sport, school, social, personal development & family).

Take ownership of your goals by sharing them with people that will help you achieve them. Coaches, parents and teammates will help keep you on track and motivate you. You cannot achieve something for someone else, and they cannot achieve it for you. Your goals have to be your own.

LOOK AT YOUR GOALS EVERY DAY – Put them on your bathroom mirror.

All three types of goals are interwoven and are all needed. In order of importance: 1) Process goals, 2) Performance goals 3) Outcome goals. By setting goals, you will achieve new heights that you never imagined possible!

List Short Term Goals:

Be specific. (how many shots I will take at home? – etc). What do you need to work on to get better? Non-hockey skills like "Focus" can be added here as well. How many pushups I will do every night? How many minutes I will run each week? Nutrition? Education – a class you need to improve?

List Medium Term Goals:

Where do I want to play next season? How to use Nationals to showcase yourself and team? What habits have I integrated into my game? What type of player do I want to become? How does my GPA affect my goals and what am I doing to ensure that I meet my educational goals as well?

List Long Term Goals:

Where do I want to play IN TWO SEASONS? Is playing Junior hockey an opportunity? Where? How? NCAA? Club? Am I training enough to keep pace with my competitors?

List team goals:

What can I do to make the team better and players around me better?

- How did I become a better player this year?
- Assess the team's performance up to this point.
- Assess your performance as a player up to this point.
- What suggestions do you have for the program for next season?
- Are you developing as much as you would like? Is there a way to improve the rate of development?

List EDUCATION Goals:

Be specific: what grades do I NEED.

What grades am I getting?

How do I achieve the grades I need?

SAT testing – what score do I need?

What other factors influence college coaches and admissions departments?

Where can I get extra help? How often?

Evaluate your Goals

As players do their part to keep on track towards their goals, it is extremely important to evaluate their plan and their skills (both tangible and intangible). Students receive feedback for schooling in the way of grades on report cards and this feedback gives students an exact evaluation.

So if teachers give feedback by way of Report Cards, coaches must also give feedback – by way of Player Evaluation meetings. Kind of like a parent teacher interview, except it is with your coach and staff. At this meeting it is critical to go over the athlete's performance in a number of areas. I have included my own Player Evaluation template in Addendum 4.

An excellent coach will walk the team and parents through the Player Evaluation form BEFORE the season and then outline when the meetings will take place. My preference for these meetings is in December before the Christmas break. The reason that December works well is that it is late enough in the season to get a comprehensive assessment of each player and it is early enough to meet with parents to go over the strengths and weaknesses of each player. This also give parents time to get "extra" help for players who are weak in a particular area. For example, if the Player Evaluation amplified that a player has a weak shot, a plan can be put in place to improve this skill.

Get ready to witness the Offenseman.

Coaches now rely on their defense to add productivity to their team's offense.

Chapter 7

The Game is CHANGING – Mostly for Defenseman

The position that is changing the most is the defenseman.

In this Chapter, I want to discuss the single most significant change in the game today – the defenseman's position. There are a ton of other changes to the way we play and teach the game so I decided to put "8 other areas of CHANGE" for specific skills into Addendum 1.

1. Puckhandling
2. Body Checking
3. Shooting
4. Passing
5. Cycling

6. Backchecking
7. Offensive Entry
8. Conditioning

New age Defending

I want to start off by examining the way defending has changed. And trust me, it has changed a lot. I devoted a whole chapter to it!

We used to have BIG, STRONG defensemen, but the game is passing these players by, and the game is now featuring defensemen who are not as big, but these players use their quick feet and their smarts – it is less about their strength. So if you want to be a great defender, big or small – you need incredible agility. Mastering agility and quickness is tough for any player. It can be especially tough for bigger players to master – but it can be done – look at Brent Burns. The NHL is featuring players that fit the quickness and smarts categories more than ever, and no longer is it a pre-requisite to be a burly, massive, strong defender who clears the front of the net. There are some giants that possess incredible agility, but the key point here is that it is <u>no longer necessary to be</u> a giant.

Generally, you have two options when defending as a defenseman: Option #1. Not to let your opponent score or Option #2. To steal the puck away from your opponent.

And let me tell you, number #2 is taking a considerably more significant role in being a good defender. To steal anything, you need great FEET. Agility, balance and quickness are keys to this skill. Think NBA players with the most steals. They anticipate their opponents move; they have the quickness to intercept. Bigger NBA defenders are doing exactly the same role as our old-school NHL defenseman, keep them to the outside, don't get let them generate a great scoring opportunity. Is that appropriate for the speed of today's game?

Today's players that dominate defending with their feet include a specific habit that also must be included in "stealing the puck." (Option #2). Defenders must have two hands on their stick at all times. Drew Doughty does this EVERY SINGLE time. He is always thinking about how to "get" the puck, not "deflect" the puck. There are seldom times when he extends his hand (one-handed) to defend.

By having two hands on the stick accomplishes another interesting feat: players do not over extend themselves with 2 hands on their stick. Instead, 2 hands allows players to be better balanced and in a better position to battle. Players that reach with one hand to prevent offensive plays are often bent over too much, and they are susceptible to cut back and skillful maneuvers by creative forwards. Drew Doughty will instead use his stick to bump the opponent's hips, trying his best to put the offensive player in an off-balance position, disabling the player's ability to create offense. Doughty uses his stick like a lacrosse stick and continually pressures the hips of the offensive player. He has no trouble getting tight to this player (eliminating space) and does not fear the cutback move. His skating agility and body position allow him to react quickly to this attempt.

The way Drew Doughty plays is new. It is different. He must have had great youth coaches that allowed him to try this unconventional style. (A lot like Bobby Orr's youth coaches who allowed Bobby to roam around the offensive zone.) This style is becoming more commonplace every year, with more and more defensive players defending a 2 on 1 with two hands on their stick. Watch and you will see defenseman accepting the rush with two hands on their stick.

Mobility is a must, but with the game getting faster, mobility is also IMPROVING at a lightning pace.

Remember it was not that long ago if you were a defenseman left in front of the net with an opposing forward, you stood between the forward and the goalie and literally tried to punish your opponent. This style is now forgotten and has been replaced with the defenseman standing in front of the forward. Two hands on the stick, trying to block shots and start a breakout. When pucks squeak by, the defense turns around and defends the offensive player with two hands, generally trying to tie up the body and stick of the opponent.

Skating

It is great to see the evolution of the game of hockey, and it is really all happening from the defenseman's position. Bobby Orr changed the game. But did he? He definitely came through a line of coaches that allowed him to be able to generate offense from the D position. He made thousands of mistakes. Many of which cost his team games from youth hockey to the NHL. But his confidence never waned. He positively impacted many more games than he negatively impacted.

Did Bobby Orr change the game? He did. But he did it solo. Subsequently, Paul Coffey followed in his footsteps, but it is astonishing how few players followed in Bobby's footsteps. What is surprising is that after Orr's career ended, few players were permitted to play an offensive skating game. Most of the best skaters continued to play forward. It seems like the youth hockey coaches from the 1980 and 1990's put every single player that possessed great skating skills on forward instead of defense. It is amazing how long it took to develop defenseman in the same mold as Bobby Orr. It wasn't until 20 years later when a couple of defensemen acquired the same amazing skating skill set as Orr, namely Bourque and Housley.

Orr and Coffey both possessed a skill superior to the rest of the league – the skating skill. My bet is that it was natural and that they didn't have full time skating coaches critiquing their every stride. And but for a few defensemen, there really hasn't been that many slick, powerful skating defenseman following in the footsteps of Orr and Coffey. Superior skating skills were reserved for forwards; Lafleur, Perreault, Gartner, Selanne, Bure, Messier, Modano – probably at least 200 superior skaters from the '80s to today. How many WERE defenseman?

No longer is it just Orr or Coffey. Or, Housley and Bourque from the 1990's or Niedermayer and Lidstrom from the 2000's (can you imagine - only 5 defenseman were picked from the 2000's out of 50 best players in the NHL AND 11 goalies were chosen!)

The skating defenseman is here now and here to stay. Here is the catch – they come with skating/skills coaches. Karrlson, Keith, Letang, Subban, Giordano, Burns, Pietrangelo, Hedman, Ellis, Fowler, Werenski, Josi, Mcdonagh, and Doughty are all among the best. This list could go on and on, but you get the idea. And the best news is - troves more are coming. Each team has one to two excellent skating defensemen. Nashville has three! And our coaches are now adjusting to allow these players to contribute offensively. And to contribute a lot!

Back to youth hockey

I believe that Bobby Orr was a forward. He saw the game offensively. He generated offense. He only lined up as a defenseman. To be honest, Bobby was a ROVER. He could play both sides of the rink. Roving will be a part of the game in 15 more years, when elite players feel just as comfortable on defense as they do on offense. IF in Parry Sound, where Bobby grew up, the teams he played on carried 6 defensemen, Bobby Orr would never have been a defenseman. Instead, he played defense, mostly because he was allowed to play at a minimum, half of each hockey game. He could probably play the entire hockey game.

So for any association that wants to create offensive, game-changing defensemen, you must allow your youth hockey teams to carry 4 defensemen. "What happens if someone gets hurt?" Forwards need to learn how to play defense. All it takes is practice. If all centers practice closing the gap, pivoting and becoming comfortable accepting the rush, every team would in essence have 4 defense and 3 extra defense (centers). So, if a defenseman on my son's team got hurt, I would want my son to stick his hand in the air for the opportunity to play defense. (If there were 4 not 6) If this was the case when I was growing up, I too might have learned to like the position – who does not want to be on the ice for half of every game? To attract the better players to play defense, there must be a carrot – if you play defense, you will play a lot more, and if you play defense, I will allow you to generate offense from this position. Music to the ears of many young players.

Creating offense from Defense

Obviously, teams are faster than they have ever been. Why are so many players getting faster? Better training. Skating coaches breaking down strides. Maximizing stride efficiency. Glide better. Smooth skating.

Skating without using your hands - "no more choo choo trains." Players skate with two hands on their stick for 95% of the game. You should train in this ratio as well. The only acceptable time to skate with one hand on the stick is "backchecking." So we should learn to skate full speed with two hands glued to our sticks, which enables us to set targets for passes, enable us to puck handle and efficiently move laterally with the puck, (think McDavid) and pass or shoot. Try doing these skills with one hand, not bloody likely.

But what does this have to do with Defenseman? D men need to be able to catch the forwards to move the puck up and SKATE. To join the attack. Defense is becoming less about playing defense and more about moving the puck quickly and catching up. 5 on 5 goals scored from offensive zone plays are a rarity. 5 on 5 goals scored on the rush, counter attacks are not the exception, rather the rule.

Dump and chase is an effective clock killer, but don't expect to generate much offense let alone score any goals. Defensemen that can skate better than the rest can find more opportunities to be a part of the offense. Turnover = GO!

Mike Babcock, coach of the Toronto Maple Leafs, uses a term "5 in a frame," and when they watch video sessions, the coach is often looking to see if all 5 players can be seen through the lens of the camera. Many times the defensemen are missing when they move the puck up the ice, but it is their job to reappear as quickly as possible. It helps two things: 1.) To attack the opponent in a group of 5 players rather than 3. 2.) It helps defense establish tight gaps with the opponent's forwards, sometimes even employing a negative gap (in front of the opponent's forwards).

Group of FIVE – how to score 5 on 5 goals

The game is changing right in front of my eyes. I see it every day. More forwards are comfortable and no longer a liability when forced into a defensive position on the ice. (Even accepting a rush.) Teams that embrace a 5 player attack will often find a rotating attack that looks more like a washing machine than a typical offensive lineup with 3 forwards working down low and the defense on the blueline.

This new style of offense is embraced by coaches like Jim Montgomery (newly appointed coach for the Dallas Stars, formerly University Denver and Dubuque USHL.) 3 championships speak of a coach that knows the game is changing and has adjusted to a style that permeates goal scoring. Jim was a scorer, and Jim wants his team to be better at offense than everyone else. To ensure this happens, the group of 5 must be retaught. Different expectations are put in place and these expectations are enormously different than their youth and junior hockey experiences. It takes time to implement this new and improved strategy because many different habits need to be replaced. A different mentality must take over the player's ingrained habits.

If you look at Jim's teams, the second half of each season is deadly, because new players have to make serious adjustments to the way offense is created. Once embraced and fear is replaced with confidence, Jim's teams bang up the score on their opponents.

Scouts. Has anyone ever heard a scout say, "wow, look at that kid play defense!" Whether a forward or defenseman, this is NOT something you hear from scouts. Ever heard this, "wow, look at that team's record!" Nope! Scouts could care less about a team's performance; they are looking for the best players and ranking their abilities. The defense can be taught. The offense can't. This is the mantra of many scouts and coaches abroad. Quite simple - it is sort of true. Sort of? Well, it is true, because teaching offense is WAY harder than teaching defense, so if I can find players that can score and understand offense, then I can coach them to play better defense. This is a fact.

The only way to get drafted is to have offensive scoring skills. Almost gone (not entirely) are the days of, "well, he has some size" and replaced with "he is small and really fast" – which player do you want to gamble on?

Defending has changed too

The defensive zone systems must evolve to keep up with the swirling attack of 5 players moving around the offensive zone. Covering your point man as a winger? Look at your point; there is nobody there! Who are you covering? Defensemen are scissoring off the blueline and attacking without the puck down to the net – unconventional yes - a coming reality? – absolutely. Teams and coaches need to figure out how to defend against this offensive style. And the reality is, that the new way to defend this style is similar to the NBA – man on man coverage. A true change from the way it has been taught for the last 00 years.

Find your man. Stay between the net and your man. Simple eh? Yeah right. It might become simpler if you picked a basketball team at tryouts. The truth is that habits are tough to change. Moreover, as coaches, we are still teaching old defensive techniques. In youth hockey the reason why we do not need to replace our offensive strategy with a new, refreshed updated one is simple – everyone can still score enough goals. In other words – the defense is still weak enough that the offense can create enough scoring chances to win hockey games.

This changes as players move up the ladder and coaches focus on the details of defending. Just a reminder, "Scouts select offensive players and teach them defense mantra". Well, defense forms the bulk of all coaching practices. Defense wins championships – huh? Yes, it does, because most coaches don't know how to coach offense. Every youth hockey coach would take the "defensive coordinator" position of a football staff, but newer, innovative, younger coaches challenge the norm and find solutions to scoring goals. Find better skating defensemen – check. Activate defensemen in the offensive zone – check. Use scissoring and screens to break down defense. Check, check.

Perfecting man to man defense has its struggles. Breakdowns caused by excellent offensive feet (think cutbacks, tight turns, hesitation moves, acceleration moves) contribute to creating space for the offense to work. In order for the defender to be successful he must not only defend the player, but watch the puck at the same time. The defense must learn to stop puck watching, while still watching the puck and player they are covering. Seems confusing – it is!

The realtime defending is complicated because of screens and picks. Success at defending begins with communication between all 5 defenders who need to work together seamlessly in a fast-paced environment. The new model offense is (using confusion and misdirection) making it extremely difficult to switch covering players...that is if you are not a basketball player. Basketball players have worked on switches their entire lives.

If you play a zone defense against a team that activates defensemen down low in the offensive zone – good luck! Many times players are left covering nobody, then the defensive player moves lower to protect the house in front of the net, which helps, but ultimately this style of defense is being left behind. All players need to know how to behave as a center down low. Switching between covering two different players is a skill. The new defender must have superior recognition skills to interpret the scenario and to communicate to the group of five on defense. Scoring will continue to escalate as coaches strive to connect the defense to a plan.

Defense – wins championships?

Not anymore.

In the 1970's and '80's NBA teams averaged between 105-110 points per game. Then the defense era began in 1990 where the team output dropped to an all-time low of 92 points per game for each team in 1998. Since then, the offense has been tweaked, players' skills have improved, and teams began the long climb back towards offensive productivity matching the '70's and '80's of 105+ points per game. Sure rule changes have enhanced offensive performance, but coaches have begun to apply the same effort toward scoring as they did towards defense. And now the NBA finally sees most games generating 200-220+ points per night. Coaches improved methods for teaching offense and offensive players skillfully practiced their outside shot to become a more lethal weapon.

The NHL is no different. Hockey was fun to watch through the '70's when team scoring was between 3.1 and 3.5 per team per game. And it was even more fun to watch and play during the '80's when scoring climbed to over 4.0 goals per team per game in the 1981/82 season, generally averaging about 3.75 goals per team per game.

Bang – "defense wins championships" – the 1990's. Worst era ever to watch hockey games. Clutching and grabbing. Hooking and fighting. More of a brawl than a hockey game. The league's worst productive season – 2.63 goals per game – in 1998, the year I played on the President's Cup (first overall in regular season) Dallas Stars team. If I turned the puck over, boom, I was headed for the press box and a healthy scratch for the next game(s). Coaches scrambled to learn the left wing lock (Detroit) or the neutral zone trap (New Jersey). It was awful hockey, but truth be told, it was amazing that the league's elite players were still able to score goals. Mike Modano single-handedly awed the fans at each game. Well, Zubie (Sergei Zubov) helped Mo a lot. I have never seen that much patience in a player with the puck than I did witnessing Zubie's ability to look attacking players off. Without Mo and Zubie, our team was very boring, but very responsible.

The trend to win championships with defense continued to the mid-2000's with rule changes coming about in 2005. Not really changes, just applying the rules! Taking out the red line was the major "change." And maybe having a closer look at goalie equipment was another great idea.

The phenomenon of defensive preached coaching = winning titles -> has been altered. An entire generation was sold a bill of goods – DEFENSE WINS. And I am not sure that this is entirely correct. What wins championships? - solid defense combined with a dynamic offense are both needed to win championships.

So here we are 12 years into the plan to score more goals. The results are in. The average went immediately from 2.57 to 3.08 as coaches learned to defend the fact that the red line was obsolete. Then scoring went on a downward trend hovering around 2.7 for 7 years in a row (2010-2016). For the 2017/18 season, teams have finally broken through and are now averaging 2.95 goals per game. Finally.

Coaches are once again beginning to focus on offense

Players from college and junior ranks are coming to the pros with a sound defensive game. Coaches are allowing defensemen to make better use of their offensive skills. Think Charlie McAvoy, Will Butcher, Shayne Gostisbehere, Noah Hannifin, Morgan Reilly – young guns who can SKATE and join the attack, always ready to contribute offensively from the back. Every team is loading up on this type of player.

College and junior coaches are looking for advantages. And scoring more goals is one that skillful coaches feel can be addressed with a system that encourages a 5 player attack. At this point in time, there are still only a handful of junior and college coaches who embrace a 5 player attack – an offensive-focused program. Soon the dinosaurs who preach defense nonstop will be extinct, and hockey will be fun to play and watch again. Soon.

"The vision of a champion is someone who is bent over, drenched in sweat, at the point of exhaustion when no one else is watching."
- Anson Dorrance

Practice starts with yourself, not your coach.

Chapter 8

Practice...we talkin 'bout practice man?

We all remember this infamous clip of Allen Iverson talking to the press about "Practice."

Practice is the most critical part of development. And, I have saved this chapter for the concluding portion of the book. A coach who becomes endeared as a "great" coach encapsulates the same qualities as a revered teacher. I want to examine the difference between a Peewee (12-year-old) coach and a grade 7 teacher.

Let's first examine the teacher.

A 7th grade teacher in the United States (middle school, 6th to 8th grade) have begun specialized teaching, similar to high school where teachers are focused on their areas of expertise. For example, a math teacher might teach several math classes. In Canada, until high school, teachers are responsible for teaching ALL of the curriculum for their students up to grade 8. Therefore they are less specialized.

BUT, all teachers are responsible for teaching a curriculum that is NOT selected by the teacher. Instead, they follow the plan that has previously been vetted and mandated by their governing body. So let's take a look at the example of math class in Grade 7. Teachers arrive early before the year begins to map out exactly how they are going to download and teach ALL of the requirements as laid out by the governing body. Teachers carefully plan how many days it will take to teach each unit, followed by a testing period. Moreover, the process repeats itself until ALL the requirements are completed by the end of the year.

However, teachers have a huge advantage over coaches. They can safely (well maybe not safely) assume that the students have spent ample time learning the foundational principles that are needed to perform the upcoming curriculum. You must pass grade 6 math to be in grade 7 math. Right?

So teachers spend a portion of each week ensuring that the students are on track to learn the entire curriculum, with the final exam as the measurement of academic success. Ever had a teacher that was behind in the curriculum and because of that, the teacher spent the last few weeks of the year teaching what was ACTUALLY going to be on the exam and absolutely no time on teaching parts of the curriculum that ARE NOT going to be on the exam? This is a result of poor planning or the result of spending too much time in one area.

Now lets' look at the Peewee Coach

More like a Canadian grade 7 teacher, the hockey coach is responsible for teaching all areas – forwards, defense and goalies all with glaring eyes (parents) continually evaluating every move. It is an incredibly tough job. Parents spend way more time getting in the business of a hockey coach than they do with their kid's grades and teachers...something is amiss here.

The association hires the coach. The coach selects a team. Now what? What skills have previously been learned? Nobody knows. What skills form the curriculum for the coming year? Nobody knows. So the main difference between a coach and a teacher is that the teacher is equipped with assumptions that are real (student passed grade 6 math) and a curriculum and timeline that must be adhered to for the upcoming year. A hockey coach has neither.

Associations must do better to help coaches; provide guidelines for expectations for everybody, coaches, players, and parents. Increased accountability starts with a great plan. I am a fan of the Association providing a Season Plan to each coach which is accompanied with the core "skills checklist." This checklist can be altered by the Association, but not by the coach. For reference, these skills checklists are in Addendum 3.

There are 3 components that go into planning a hockey season:

1. Season Plan
2. Block Plan
3. Practice Plans

These components serve to make the season a great success and keep all parties interested in what is going on in any particular timeframe. I have found that parents get a lot out of a well thought out Plan. Moreover, respect climbs for a coach who is purposefully thinking about how to break down his expectations of teaching the players.

1. Season Plan

This is a summary of the expectation for the upcoming season. This Plan can be tweaked by the coach, but the main pieces are dictated by the Association. Included areas for covering consist of:

- Practice times and frequency per week
- Game schedule
- Tournaments – dates and destinations
- Dryland / Off-ice Training
- Fitness testing, on and off the ice
- Video Training - frequency
- Summer Training
- Goalie Training
- Player / Parent – Evaluation meetings

- Goal Setting
- Team Expectations
- The budget as a total – no breakdown of the budget until you become a member of the team.

Typically this plan is in point form and topically discusses the expectations of parents and players, most importantly – the budget is revealed. The Season Plan also sets in motion the answers to many questions that prospective parents want to know. What is the time commitment, budget, etc.? When speaking to a prospective player, coaches can send the Season Plan as an outline that describes -> what playing for a coach like you entails.

Once tryouts are finished, and the team is selected, I like to deliver to the parents a second, more detailed Season Plan – INTERNAL. In this Plan, I like to break down the Budget and get more specific about the plan for each of the bullets.

2. Block Plans

After tryouts, I like to think about the Season as a whole and the curriculum that I need to teach. To keep on track and "building" towards the end of the season, coaches should consider dividing the season into BLOCKS. I like blocks as opposed to segments because we are building a player upwards, like Jenga!

Coaches can consider different timeframes for the season for designating when a BLOCK begins and ends. For example, a Peewee Hockey coach should take into consideration the skills that must be taught over the course of the season, highlighting a smaller list of skills that will become the focus of Block One. I find it useful to use between 5-6 Blocks over the course of a year. (Think tests as a teacher). When you highlight skills for say a 10 practice period, (Block period) it will help you deliver a better practice plan to the players which give the players enough time to work on the skills. These skills will overlap into future blocks, so it is not critical to master the skill, rather it is critical to understand the skill and how the skill applies to a game situation.

Think of a BLOCK as a way of keeping coaches on track to teaching the entire curriculum. The fun part of being the coach is that coaches get to select from the checklist whatever skills a coach feels is necessary for each BLOCK. Blocks can be formed well ahead of the season. They are merely an outline of what the players will be learning over a period of time. Here is an example of 5 Block Plan periods:

Block ONE – training camp to our first tournament (October 5)
Block TWO – October 7 – November 15
Block THREE – November 16 - Christmas Break (Dec 20)
Block FOUR – January 2 – February 15
Block FIVE – February 15 to end of Season

Feel free to add more blocks or reduce them, but it is essential to write out how the skills will be learned and when they will be learned.

3. Practice Plans

Some coaches love this part, some not so much. These plans are the lifeblood of a team. Coaching takes a ton of time. Most of us spend WAY too much time planning, but we do it because we love it. Planning for a great practice is fun. However, what we need to do as coaches is to understand how to plan a practice! What? "I thought I knew how to do this!"

What are the skills that I need to teach this Block? What did I write in my BLOCK PLAN? And if I begin the first week of the month with a BottomUP plan, then move to TOPDown – self-guided plan, the probability of players forming habits goes through the roof. The player's ability to execute without thinking sky rockets!

Practice planning is a skill. The skill is in planning while keeping the long-term vision in mind.

The Practice Plans detail precisely what will happen for each practice. Details include:
- Equipment needed: pylons, tires, nets, dividers, etc.
- Coaches – expectations, flow – from one drill to the next
- Time for each drill
- Number of players
- Drill – purpose and teaching points

12U Practice 25.26   *Time:* 60 Minutes   **Number of Players:** 30+

Equipment: 9 Cones, 6 Tires, Dividers, Ringette Rings, Extra Sticks, 4 Nets

Warm Up: 8 minutes
Players pair up with one puck per pair. On the whistle, play 1v1 keep away with their partner. Have players stay in a confined area attempting to stickhandle around or through their partner. Play for 40 seconds, rest for 40 seconds. On the whistle to rest, players stand 15' apart and pass to one another. Forehand passes, backhand passes, and bullet passes (pass as hard as possible). Have players pass cross body and sweep the puck. Coaches correct technique.

Stations: 3 Stations x 10 minutes

Agility: Half Burpees (squat, plank, stand...)

Station 1: Puck Control – Deception
Use rings and pucks – controlled exaggerated movements.
A. Using rings make wide exaggerated moves to forehand and backhand. Emphasis on knee bend and loading legs.
B. Exaggerated moves using pucks
C. Exaggerated moves sliding under stick
D. 1v1 shuttle, attack triangle, against passive players

Station 2: Stops, Starts, Transition Skating
Skating skills technique, stop and start at each cone (head and chest up). Progress to forward to backwards pivots. Add in agility at the red line (drop to knees and up) and then add in pucks.

Station 3: 1v1 Competitions
Players compete 1v1 for 30 second shifts. Coaches add in additional pucks if a goal is scored or goalie covers it. Rotate after each shift to next area, 1 to 2, 2 to 3, 3 to 1. (Use a tire as a goal if not enough goalies or nets)

Game: 3v3 with Outlets – 10minutes
Play 3v3 cross-ice for 40 second shifts. Players must make a pass to one of the coaches (outlets) on transition before they can score. Use tires for goals if not enough goals or goalies. Play 3 different 5 minute games using rotation mentioned above.

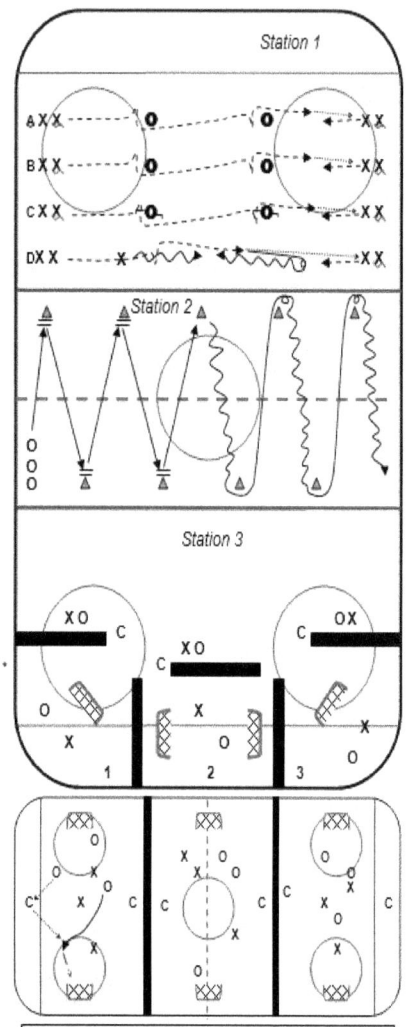

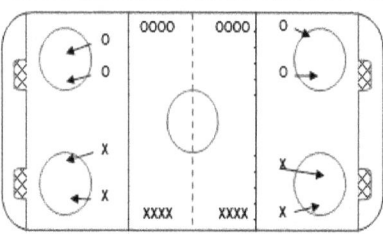

Competition: 10 Puck Quick Score- 10min
Teams line up along the boards at each blueline, 5 pucks are laid out on the blue line for each team. Players attack the net 2 v0 and go until they score. Once they score they sprint out of the zone over the blue line at which point the next 2 v0 begins. Teams play until all 5 pucks are scored, first team to score all 5 of their pucks wins!

Have a look at a USA Hockey – Peewee Practice Plan. I like to date my plans and have them ready to look at later.

Practice Planning – Bad Habits

Here is what I mean: It is October. Do I let the results of last game decide what I teach in practice? I hope not. How much time is wasted in the 60 minute practice? Is there too much coach talk? Do I waste time allowing players to stretch on the ice? ONE LAP! When a coach feels the urge to yell "one lap" at the conclusion of each drill/situation, this really means that the coach needs to have a minute to think about what is coming up next. Consider what is going to happen next before the drill/situation concludes, so that when the whistle blows, players can immediately move to the next scenario / situation.

Practice Planning – GREAT Habits

- Plan is either sent out to players ahead of time or posted in the dressing room
- The plan uses NAMED drills. A good idea is to name drills after players on your own team.
- Assistant coaches know their responsibility and actively help transition from one situation to the next
- Rotation is clear
- Timeframe is clear – this can be tweaked shorter/longer as the situation is being absorbed
- Always have ONE too many drills/situations – it is always easy to cut a drill out

Great Thoughts

- Cognitively, how are my players learning? Do they understand the concept being delivered?
- Less teaching moments – understand the benefit of delayed feedback often referred to as: Summary Feedback
- Do the situations utilize self-guided discovery?
- Do the drills/situations have competitiveness?
- Do the drills/situations have multiple decision-making components?

You know you are doing a great job when your players are asking you questions. They are thinking about what they are doing and they are taking ownership in their improvement.

Deliberate Practice

Don't forget the deliberate practice methods, ensuring that players are constantly being pushed to the edge of their abilities. Keeping the rate of failure high by creating situations that are difficult to solve.

Coaches must remember that players need to be cognitively engaged, which really means that players must be able to have multiple outcomes to each situation. Solving problems every step of the way. Rate your drills and practice by asking yourself, "how many minutes did my players solve problems during my practice?"

Make Hockey Great Again

Hey hockey enthusiasts, I hope you are enjoying my book so far.

I have a favor to ask you. Would you please consider giving it a rating on Amazon, please?

My goal is to help hockey coaches, players and parents everywhere and for this book to be a corner piece in the bookcase of every player and coach.

The social media impact in our society is incredible, so if you like it, a few tweets would help a ton,
hash tags #makehockeygreatagain
www.makehockeygreatagain.com
Twitter – mike_kennedy39
Instagram – instagram.com/goldstandardhockey
Facebook – facebook.com/makehockeygreatagain
LinkedIn – linkedin.com/makehockeygreatagain

Thanks a ton, *Mike*

Chapter 9

The REAL question is...HOW?

What can we do to increase athletic success?

The first thing I think we can agree on is that reducing the space for the players will increase the speed of decision making. And by placing a set of rules into the "playing area game" will further enhance a player's ability to intelligently solve a particluar situation that the coach identifies for development. The key is to develop creative, highly skilled players who habitually find ways to "solve" difficulties encountered.

Skill is not enough. Aptitude is not enough. A coach's ability is mixing skill and aptitude together. What effects of the training will transfer to competition performance for the LONG TERM?

So once again – how?

The first part is that we as coaches, parents and administrators must look at what method performs best over the LONG run. There are two methods that I would like to explain in greater detail. The first, the "Bottom Up Approach."

The Bottom Up and Top Down Approaches

I like to read and learn about how all coaches think, not just hockey coaches. And most of the information that I come across sets the table for "what we should be doing." The problem is that I rarely learn something about HOW. So in this chapter, the focus will change to HOW we can better positively impact our young athletes.

Bottom Up

As a young athlete, there are two methods by which we can learn to execute a skill. The first, known as bottom-up theory uses the following approach: Disassemble the skill. Break it down. Demonstrate the techniques. Add a lot of feedback. Correction analysis. Add in difficulty – more speed. Repeat. This is a common coaching practice that is widely used across North America to help our athletes get better. This is like hiring an instructor to help teach your son/daughter to ride a bike.

Top Down

The second approach known as the top down theory is heavily focused on self-guided discovery. Forget teaching the exact movements, instead concentrate on the shaping of the practice to allow players to discover and execute a skill on their own. This does not mean that we abandon feedback and criticism. Instead, we urge and promote players to learn skills on their own.

There is a big difference between these two styles. Learning through self-guided discovery ensures the transfer of the skills will be inserted into games. And when I say skills – I mean little things like – getting open for a pass.

A player who fails and succeeds often improves the quickest. Failing is key. For hockey players – think playing on the pond or outdoor hockey with no coaches. Trial and error is all that exist and when failure turns the corner and success arrives – look out!

ALWAYS HAVE THE ATHLETES COGNITIVELY BE ENGAGED.

Example: I spend hours breaking down the toe drag. A move that at younger age levels can become quite a skillful maneuver and can lead to offensive chances. I talk about the hand position, the puck position and how to entice a defender to take a swipe/poke at the puck. In an instant, the puck is dragged backwards, while maintaining forward skating. The puck is then pulled forward, and the forward escapes the clutch of the defender and leaves the defender in the dust. Hours of practice. Execution levels rises. The skill is becoming mastered. Great.

Example: I spend a couple of minutes showing the skill and then put the players into a shaped environment of 2 on 2 or 3 on 3. Even 1 on 1. And they play and play and play. And I continue to focus the attacking player making a "toe drag" play – or NOT. This move has timing to it; you can't do the move every time. I might show a toe drag on video of Jonathon Toews or Jordan Eberle – watch – copy...Learn on your own. Learn the timing. Learn the signals coming from the defender. Put the puck in a position to entice the defender to swipe at the puck. Failure. Repeat. There are not enough words or feedback you can give to master this skill, rather, players who learn it on their own will find that they "don't really know what exactly they are doing or seeing, rather a sensational 'feel' comes to mind and the skill is purely – executed."

The two examples above set out a philosophy – one is a completely controlled environment, unlike a hockey game, and one is shaped into an environment that is conducive for practicing the move. Want to know what else? The environment that is shaped can have more than one teaching point. Practicing multiple moves, pucks through feet, pucks through the triangle, change of speed, pucks handled outside the body -> are all examples of offensive skills that can be practiced and repeated in the exact same "shaped environment" that was intended for the toe drag skill.

Here is what we know about BottomUP and TOPDown. Younger kids will benefit more from the BottomUP and coaches that use this style to teach will give their teams an advantage for the first few years. However, coaches that really understand the word – DEVELOPMENT, won't worry about the score of each game of 6-10-year-old hockey and instead embrace the philosophy of TOPDown and encourage this style of shaping practices with environments that lean towards self-discovery. Pretty soon the TOPDown coaches will reap the rewards by seeing skills being executed as habits – the best you can ask for as a coach.

I talked about a toe drag but think about this for a moment… Early stage development includes skating around tons of cones, edges are being formed, and players can see their own improvements coming quickly. However, what if instead, players continued to play 1 on 1, 2 on 2, 2 on1 – edges are also being built, success and failures are being processed, and players are also having tons of fun. I am not saying to get rid of your cones entirely, but consider this – equalize the time between cones and playing. Move from the cones into an environment that is shaped around playing, rules to the games can enhance the specific skill that is being focused on. A drill that I loved coaching and playing was racing around a few cones to a loose puck. Playing a 1 on 1 until the coach blew the whistle. The race + the competition = FUN.

Deliberate Practice

This term comes from a book called the Talent Code. It will change how you think as a coach. The premise of the book is that Talent exists in combination with extremely focused effort. What I like best about this book is that the role of the coach must become his/her ability to find ways to get the players to practice in a "deliberate" way. Basically what it means is to practice on the edge of your abilities. You can replace 10 hours of practice with 1 hour of deliberate practice. It is a challenging task to undertake, but it needs to be strived for by coaches.

If hockey is expensive to play, then we need to focus on how to get more "deliberate" practices in a season. A lot more.

The goal here is to embrace the kids who want hockey to be their primary focus – their passion. Yes, keep them playing soccer, baseball, lacrosse – whatever, but when the time comes to focus on hockey – our dryland, off-ice training can still be focused on being an ATHLETE, not a hockey player.

When we learn to coordinate our hands by shooting a basketball, or spiking a volleyball, our hardware (the body) allows faster downloads of the software (brain) skills. By becoming a better "athlete" players can more swiftly accelerate the software by learning to execute skills more quickly.

Players that want to go a long way in hockey can simply adopt the Steffi Graf approach: she scored the absolute highest score when measuring her competitive desire and her ability to sustain concentration along with the ability to run!

Make Hockey Great Again

Embrace Challenges.

Persistence is key.

Effort is the pathway to all achievement.

Chapter 10

The TRUTH

No player knows their ultimate ceiling.

Without a doubt this chapter has been the toughest to complete. The final chapter represents a collection of the most important pieces of this book, and the objective is to leave you with a renewed sense of purpose.

I want to keep this chapter short (yet it still has six parts) so that the message is as clear as possible and I want to make sure that coaches, parents, and players can refer to this chapter for the rest of their hockey careers, so here goes:

Part 1. Hockey is FUN.

The number ONE reason hockey is fun is that we like to play! Outdoor hockey / shinny / Stick and Puck (whatever you call it) – a place where players quickly form teams and start a game all on their own! <u>*UNCOACHED*</u> – is that a new word? Is it possible that Auston Matthews perfected those unbelievable hands away from his coaches and on the 3 on 3 rink? My answer is yes. Skills coaches help modify and enhance techniques, but the practice and development of the skills are best suited to be learned in a repetitive environment with 1,000's of attempts. (In small areas you get way more attempts!)

As players, we all look forward to the games, so when we develop our players during practices using situations that look a lot like a game – players and coaches BOTH win! Not only are small area games (SAG) good for players to develop their decision-making skills, these games also benefit the players tremendously because they are enjoyable to play. So that leads us into Part 2.

Part 2. Small Area Games – Development and FUN

If you adopt a small area game for a "station" that runs all practice long (possibly for an entire season) here is what you will develop without much coaching:

- Edges, stops, tight turns, bursts of speed to loose pucks, body position on loose pucks

- Passing - finding correctly or incorrectly endless options: forehands, backhands, saucers they all come into these games
- Shooting - scoring chances should form a massive part of small area games, wrist shots, backhands, wrap arounds, tips, deflections, pouncing on rebounds – what more do you want?
- Puck protection – playing defense is the grueling part of playing small area games and to rectify having to play defense, players learn to keep possession of the puck and expose the puck to turnovers less often – another great skill (think NHL 3 on 3)
- Goalie attention - shots, playing the puck, passing the puck, poking at the puck, covering rebounds – wow – all the skills goalies need to work on in an environment that simulates actual game play.
- Then there is the cognitive development – situational awareness. 2 on 1, read – pass or shoot. Make the defense mess up with fakes and misdirection. Players learn how creating a "small" advantage leads to a scoring chance. And learning how to exploit an advantage quickly, are all part of cognitive development.
- Defending – small area games work best when points are awarded. Coaches can define the game and score points based on concepts that are to be addressed.

Much like a real game, there is a winner and loser. Consider the losing team doing a rollover or two pushups; there should be a consequence of losing and this consequence really ramps up the intensity. Nobody likes to lose even if it is only 2 pushups.

Where does hockey sense come from? For some players, it may be an inborn trait, but for most players, hockey sense comes through experience. If they are not on the outdoor rinks playing pick-up hockey, where is that experience going to come from? It comes from games, but the difficulty is that players play only 15 minutes each per game, with only 20 seconds of puck time. So the answer is that the experience must come through small area games in practice. Virtually any individual or team skill can be taught through the use of small-area games.

Can coaches teach "hockey sense?" The answer is YES. Moreover, the reason is that constantly putting players in small areas will quickly enhance their problem-solving abilities. No more patterns on the ice with timing that the coaches insist on. Instead, play Small Area Games which limit decision-making TIME and enhance hockey IQ. Players need to be constantly put into situations with opposition. No more skating around without solving a problem. "Thinking" skills need to be developed. Failure must be constant. Success is looming. If you play often with limited time, these scales will eventually be flipped to success being constant and failure fading away.

Part 3. TALENT IS OVERRATED.

And in fact, the word "talented" in sports or any other craft is a copout. A word used by people that express a bewilderment complimented with awe. The word has a double-edged sword associated with it – on one end, the "talented" player becomes aware of the awe, and the player sees his natural ability to be the driver of success and relinquishes the work ethic required to stay on top. On the other end of the sword, many athletes become discouraged when putting in the same amount of time as the "talented" player yet these players do not achieve the same success which can lead to becoming less determined.

So if Talent is overrated, and work ethic reigns true, we must remember that the other key to incredibly high achievement is: SUSTAINED OBSESSION. And let's all face the facts, if your kid is good at Fortnite, (video games) he/she likely won't be the best in his class at hockey. See, for superstars (AHL players and beyond is my definition for superstars), their talent and willpower to get better supercedes every other option. For youth, there are many options to pull you away from your obsession and if your son or daughter is being pulled away – the obsession can be likened to this statement: Am I along for the ride, or am I "all-in." It is quite all right to be along for the ride. Not every player wants to be elite. So if you don't want to be elite, there are still many great reasons to being a youth hockey player. You don't have to be elite to learn a ton of life lessons about comradery and teamwork, but if you want to be the best, there are sacrifices you have to make. I need to change the word – ~~sacrifices~~ there are <u>choices</u> you have to make. Becoming great is a CHOICE.

Remember, early success is not a predictor of future long-term achievement. There are hundreds of stories of athletes not being the best at a high school age group and yet are unrelenting in their quest to master their craft only later to be rewarded. These athletes have an even greater gift – work ethic equals success, and these athletes never forget what got them to the top.

In the book Champions Mind, by Jim Afremow, Jim leads us down the path of Excellence as seen through the eyes of Anson Dorrance, Women's NCAA Soccer Coach – EXCELLENCE - He (Anson) was driving to work early one morning, and as he passed a deserted field, he noticed one of his players off in the distance doing extra training by herself. He kept driving, but he later left a note in her locker: "The vision of a champion is someone who is bent over, drenched in sweat, at the point of exhaustion when no one else is watching." The young woman, Mia Hamm, would go on to become one of the best women's soccer players in the history of the sport.

From the player's side, the ability to see failure as a critical component to future success is massive towards their development. As an athlete, how can you push past the stigma of falling down? In fact – falling down is a requirement to accelerated learning. To put in another way – you must practice on the EDGE

OF YOUR ABILITIES at all times. And if you do, you will be falling down often. An example of falling down/failing could be this: during your shot, you try to release the puck with your head up, you pull the puck towards your feet and bend your stick to boomerang the puck towards the net – AND then - only ice chips fly. The puck has squirted just off the end of your stick and you have WHIFFED totally. (Shooting this way is an easy skill to perform by looking down, perhaps only a glance downwards – but at higher levels, that single glance can be the difference between making it or not). So keep whiffing. Trust me, it goes away!

This is just like a gold medal figure skating champion – falling down 20,000 times and each one causing a bruise, and in front of her coach and peers. The determination to nail it and move on without one single thought of failure. Instead, each failure was a step on a long staircase that ends with getting to the top. How many times are you willing to fall down? Miss the puck? Close the gap too much? Come out of your net to play pucks? Just a few examples...

In order to achieve – players must maintain their eagerness to learn and grow. Take all information thrown at you. Growth Mindset is putting accountability on your own future. From physical training to mental toughness, elite players need to be self-determined to get better.

Pat Riley once said, "The attitude a person develops is the most important ingredient in determining the level of success." You must be committed to continually improving yourself. The journey to achieving better performance is a sure thing when you can do that.

I watched a USHL training camp in Las Vegas and saw my pal, Dane Jackson there scouting a midget player from the west coast. And let me tell you, this player had a ton of skill. I knew who he was. Like top in the age group for skating, skill and size. Anyway after an hour, I asked Dane, "so what do you think?" to which Dane replied, "he is not a North Dakota player." Wow! I mean how good do you have to be? Dane saw the player's character as the biggest drawback. In particular, the player's lack of desire to fight for pucks that were turned over. Good players turn the puck over. But which good player is relentlessly wiling to get the puck back? There are pretenders and then there are the players that Dane is looking for.

Part 4. Coaching.

If Talent is Overrated for athletes, is the same true for coaches? To become a "talented" coach it takes a ton of experience. Many former pros have the "experience" yet make lousy youth hockey coaches because they don't know how to articulate what they want to teach and they don't understand the vast amount of preparation time it takes to be a great youth hockey coach. Teaching is not easy; it is a skill that is honed and improved over time. Top coaches are just as obsessed as players in their quest to keep learning. A great coach is one who is obsessed with preparation and dialed in on the details that can tilt the odds in his favor.

A great coach is always on the lookout for ways to keep accelerating the learning for players and to keep the learning as enjoyable as possible.

Here is the definition of a "talented" coach: A coach who realizes his/her purpose is to TEACH. (And as John Wooden says, "you haven't taught until they have learned.") Further, as teacher, the coach must also continue to learn. Mike Babcock is famous for his roundtables of asking successful youth and junior coaches', "what is YOUR key to team success?" and then Mike is studying the coaches answers for anything that he might be able to "steal" and use for himself. That is the purpose of a roundtable – not to lead the horses to water, but to drink with the horses.

The volume of effort and time required to be put in each and every season is unbelievable. So a detailed PLAN can help keep you organized and on track. Only when the plan has been meticulously put together will all the pieces fall into place. Remember the details of planning – use training blocks to keep on schedule and learn to set out your priority for each practice!

When putting practice plans together, coaches should focus on "situation" training. Moreover, when you do this, practice will feel like a game. Cut out patterns on the ice? Replace this with patterns that happen in a game. How does a 2 on 1 actually happen in a game? Surely a backchecker is coming, and quick decision-making is paramount – shoot or pass for the forwards, taking space away from the shooter or forcing an errant pass for the defense? Recreate these scenarios in practice – all the way through the actual attempt – there will likely be one of 4 results: 1. Goal. 2. Rebound. 3. Save. 4. Missed shot / missed pass.

PLAY IT OUT!

Everything I have read (and it feels like I have read an entire library) on the topic of Skill Development comes down to this: Show them (demonstrate), allow a few practice repetitions and then set up situations (small area games) where the players can focus on the intended skill – with opposition!!! Whatever the skill, the quickest way to accelerate the development is to ADD OPPOSITION. Sticks upside down, no sticks for defenders, and fewer defenders are all excellent variables. When players learn skills in this type of environment, the coach will be rewarded by seeing this skill performed in a game. This is the complete opposite of learning a skill with ZERO opposition where the skill stands alone – and stays in practice, never to be seen in a game. By having opposition, players are forced into failing – a key requirement for future success. Some players will show an aptitude for the skill, and some players will take more time to perform the skill successfully – it doesn't always take 20,000 fails! No matter what, players who perform the skill easily should be confined to smaller spaces and more opposition.

Part 5. Parenting Better

As a parent, you know you have an athlete with sustained obsession when you don't have to ask your kid to shoot pucks in the garage. Instead, you have to keep repairing the garage, net, house, parked car, appliances, drywall... you get the idea. Alternatively, if your player wakes you up at 6am instead of the other way around – you know you have an obsessed player. Lastly, young players who watch a lot of hockey are obsessed. Creativity, execution and dazzling skills can all be stolen by watching the best players in the world as closely as a poker player holds his cards.

Whether or not your player is obsessed, each young hockey player needs to learn how to be GRITTY. Grit – "the willpower to persevere with passion and a sense of purpose." Wow, what an exceptional habit to hold onto for your entire life. Darrin Donnelly writes in his book titled, Grit, "how to never give up and never back down in the face of life's biggest challenges." And Darrin further explains, "People today are, in general, much more likely to quit at something than they used to be. They're much less persistent. Even if it's something they enjoy and are good at, they throw in the towel much faster than they once did. They expect things too easy and they get easily frustrated by setbacks."

Athletes need parents to help them learn that GRIT is being responsible for yourself and the outcomes that occur. It is up to each player to determine for himself/herself how to respond to a negative event like being cut from a team. Does being cut make you more determined than ever? Is more effort required? How much more?

Grit is coming to the rink every day with an attitude that screams to everyone, "I am here to get better, and I am not wasting a single moment in my desire to achieve this." When players refuse to let a moment go by, their dreams are always one inch closer.

When a player is encouraged by his parents to take an attitude that pushing himself/herself to the edge of his/her abilities is paramount to accelerating development.

Chasing a big dream is easy. Overcoming the hurdles is tough. Keep positive. Keep encouraging. Understand obsession. Teach persistence. Getting knocked down and then getting back up again is what success is always about.

As a parent, ensure that hockey is always fun. When you do these things, you will notice that the competitors will begin to fade away.

Part 6. And Finally – New age Defense.

It is extremely important to develop players in every position, after all, hockey is fairly simple -> skate, pass, shoot. There are a ton of other skills that go into being a great hockey player, but don't you think that if you can do those three skills pretty well, that it shouldn't matter where you line up on the ice?

For younger players up to 13 years old, it is wise to develop as a player in every position. I even recommend goalies to play out as a player (especially in spring hockey). The game is not as complicated as some coaches make it. Get used to having pressure, and get used to finding solutions to each problem presented. The reason forwards struggle on defense and vice versa, is that we don't have enough experience to lean on to make smart decisions. No better way to get more experience than to be both a forward and defense in all practice scenarios.

As players get older (past 14), each player should be focusing on three things as a defender: 1. Continually defend with an aggressive gap which needs to lead to failing 50% of the time. By failing often, you will hasten the pace of learning and calculating the correct distance to close gaps. 2. Once the puck has moved up the ice to a forward – if you can skate PAST a forward, then you become a forward for the remainder of the shift. This small rule will really lead defensemen to get up the ice and join the attack. There will be some defensive setbacks because of this, but that is what offensive coaching is all about -> teaching players to read the play and sometimes cover for the attacking defenseman. 3. When defending in your own end, always think like Drew Doughty, "how can I get this puck FROM the offensive player?" and refrain from thinking, "how can I deflect this puck away?" One situation involves two hands and great feet, the other involves slower feet and an outreached hand.

All coaches need to put some time and effort into seeing how the game is transitioning to a 5 player offensive juggernaut that when looking from above is hard to tell just which player is a forward and which player is a defenseman.

To get a great picture of what I mean, try typing these two URL's into your browser:

1. **https://tinyurl.com/yb8wm6j9**

   Watch Buffalo... wow, that is the way the NEW cycle happens and finishes with a "slight" interference scissor which lets Jack Eichel rip a shot from the slot and score. FYI: Also, watch how the LA Kings defenders are taught to play defense against this style. Hint – it ain't the old school way!

2. **https://tinyurl.com/y8faupro**

   Watch Chicago, this clip begins with a set faceoff play and then turns into a great indicator of how the game is changing. And man, is this FUN to play! Playing Defense becomes a lot more fun!

If you like these clips – be sure to subscribe to my YouTube Channel! **https://tinyurl.com/y9varhuf**
"Tinyurl" takes you to the main page of my YouTube channel and you can see the 100+ video of faceoff plays, fakes, scissors, defending and much more.

If as a coach, player or parent, if you could take just one single impression from this book,

– this would be it:

Coach - Replace the word "Drills" with "SITUAITONS." That way, you can be sure that your practice will be similar to a game with players continuously facing opposition.

Player - Talent is overrated, to become great is a choice.

Parent - Teach your children to be gritty. Those with the growth mindset find setbacks motivating.

The journey to get better never ends.

Thank you for reading, let's stay connected.

Coach Mike

A set of Addendums are included in this book and they address areas of further insight that I hope each reader enjoys.

Addendums

1. Updated Hockey Skill Sets

I decided to put an addendum together that further explained the way that skills are being taught.

There are definitely more changes than the ones listed here in this book, but I thought this would be a good start. Here is a list of skills that have evolved:

1. Puckhandling – tied directly to VISION
2. Body Checking
3. Shooting – The wrister is KING
4. Passing – Old vs New School
5. Cycling – the '80s way vs today
6. Backchecking – Ken Hitchcock redefined this
7. Offensive Entry – Time to get Creative
8. Conditioning – during practice!
9. Skill Building

1. Puckhandling – tied to VISION

This is an overlooked skill and coaches at every level must pay more attention to improving this skill, including NCAA and CHL levels.

Many kids use their bottom hand like they would on a lacrosse stick, letting it slip around the glove and therefore letting the top hand do all the work. The bottom hand is extremely important, and both hands must work in unison. The game is too fast to let the stick slip, and the recovery will be too late to make a play. To rectify this, players should practice stick handling with no gloves on and watch your bottom hand roll in unison with the top hand.

Hands are way closer today. And I think it is because of the speed of the game. There is no time to reposition your hands to shoot the puck. (WRISTERS) So players must learn to puck handle and shoot the puck from in front of their body.

Forwards have adapted to the speed and have learned that it is quicker to shoot the puck from the front leg also from the puck handling position than it is to bring the puck backward and release it off a long runway in order to achieve power. Alos, when you move your hand slightly lower and deliver a "traditional wrist shot" (I joke about taking 10 minutes to get off) allows everyone to know the shot is coming. The goalie knows, the defense knows, everyone in the rink knows you are shooting.

So puck handling and shooting go together. I grimace when I see kids rear the puck back. It just won't work in a game, yet we still practice this shot all the time. Seems counterproductive to me. Even for a six-year-old, shoot the puck from in front of your body. Once the habit of bringing the puck back forms, it is difficult to break.

The players with the most exceptional vision have the best puck handling abilities. Think Kane, Crosby, McDavid, Matthews. These players move the puck back and forth on their blade so quickly it is mind-blowing. Vision is tied to puck handling. The better you can feel the puck on your blade, feel its smoothness, feel it when the puck is at the toe or heel and when it is perfectly in between. This is the "glue" - that centrifugal force that allows a player's head to be in a vision gathering mode. Most players can skate and puck handle and most can even do it with their head up. Once again, the skill has been fairly mastered, but also once again, is this player able to use incredible vision in a game? Think of a player rushing the puck through the neutral zone – what type of vision does this player have? Great players see in front, to the sides and even look back to capture images of what the possibilities could be as they navigate the puck through the neutral zone. Should I slow down and let a teammate catch up to outnumber an opponent? The possibilities are endless.

Can you do this in a game? At full speed? With players attacking you? Are you able to see the "whole" ice? Most players cannot do this, and we do not spend enough time teaching this "vision" skill. But the truth of the matter lies in the puckhandling skills, if you need to glance (eye flick) down at the puck, you need more practice! And the only way to get better at this skill is if you "lose" the puck and repeat. Start the puckhandling skills skating more slowly, and advance the skills by adding speed and "moving obstacles" that create a game like feel. Cones will not do the trick.

I also want players and coaches to emphasize moving the puck and shooting it. This is a puckhandling skill tied into shooting. There are a ton of variations to this, but the basic concept is the same – always pretend there is a defender trying to block your shot. Be more creative when shooting. Drag shoot, pull shoot, fake shoot, push shoot, backhand to forehand shoot, shoot off the stickhandle: all important ways to shoot.

2. Body Checking – New School

Incidentally, as I begin this section, I would like to see "open ice" body checks eliminated from youth hockey. Yes, stand someone up strongly, but to use excessive force – for what? The purpose of body checking is twofold:

1. To separate the man from the puck; and

2. To eliminate your opponent from getting into the potential play.

I played in Germany's DEL league for 6 years and we always had a good chuckle when our defense rocked an opposing player in the neutral zone and our defense was always called for some kind of penalty- we called it "hitting too hard." And in youth hockey these body checks, while legal, should be eliminated.

Body checking's do's and don'ts are still pretty much the same, with the exception of this:

Old School – teach the player to take a rounded, curved route to the puck which will put the player in a safer position. As coaches, we call it "angle" towards the puck.

New School – if you take the former path (Old School), forecheckers are likely to beat you to the puck. Instead, head directly towards the puck and begin to slow down as you approach the puck. Make sure the player you are racing with is between the puck and you. You may have to alter your route to ensure this. As you get 10 feet from puck lean into your opponent. The play is to "take a hit" but also, move the puck to your defense partner, or reverse to the winger, just before taking the hit. So, lean on the opponent, 2 hands on your stick and play the puck while absorbing the hit. The hit will never be too bad, as you have absorbed the speed of your opponent and slowed considerably.

3. Shooting – The wrister is KING

Wow has shooting changed a lot! The slapshot is pretty much dead. The quick release wrist shot is king. Even top tier defensemen are using the quick release wrist shot more and more.

The other important shot to learn from a young age is the one-timer. Constant practice will make this shot more effective. Some key points to taking great one-timers – keep your shoulders loose. Your upper body should be as square to the puck as possible. Keep your hands loose as well, a tight grip won't help!

The timing comes from smashing the puck from the middle of your blade. And a steep downward swing is what will create flex on your stick as you smash your blade into the ice a fraction ahead of when the puck arrives. This will allow the flex to add velocity to the puck. If you hit the puck towards the heel, the result will be one-timers that scream across the ice; if you hit it towards the toe, the shot will flutter like a wounded duck. It is important to practice this shot while moving (think 2 on 1 receptions) and one timing pucks from areas just above the goal line that often come as rebounds!

THE WRIST SHOT is the most important shot in hockey. From youngsters who are just learning to pro's who can pick the corners, this shot is the goal scoring shot for forwards.

Times have changed and so has the way a wrist shot is taken. Gone are the days of the long runway, reach back and slingshot the puck forward. The game is too fast for this type of shot now and it is important to get youth hockey players to shoot the puck correctly from a young age.

There are actually two types of wrist shots. The first and more traditional (old school / stationary) shot happens when you move the leg that is closest to the blade of your stick in the opposite direction of the puck while keeping balance on the outside leg. This shot is useful and has more accuracy and power attached to it. Its flaw is that it takes longer to get the shot off and goalies are more accustomed to seeing it.

THE SECOND SHOT happens when you lean on your inside leg and lift your outside leg allowing the player to put pressure on the stick and create flex, sometimes called shooting of the "off" foot. Or what I call the "Kessel" shot. This shot is typical of the way Phil Kessel shoots. To make this shot powerful, athletes must lean heavily on their stick. Phil keeps his head low and transfers his upper body weight across the stick and blade which creates a big whip. He is able to shoot the puck extremely quickly from the same spot he stick handles from. His top hand is way out in front of his body and he actually PULLS back on the top hand. This shot is tough for goalies to read and tough for defenders to block because of the short amount of time it takes to take this shot.

Important features of a good stick:

STICK SIZE

Many parents are too quick to move up in stick size. The easy rule is that at least two fingers must touch the palm when you wrap your hand around the stick. If there is any space, the stick is too big in circumference.

LENGTH

The old fashioned rule is between your chin and nose, but that has long been abolished. For crafty, puck handling players, a shorter stick usually prevails. Marty St. Louis' (a crafty Hart Trophy winner) stick was above his head. I believe in trying different lengths to see what your personal preferences are. Start longer and cut is a good way to go!

CURVE

Once again the curve is a fun way for players to try different sticks. Have fun trying shots with different curves and as long as you can do a decent backhand, I endorse all types of curves.

4. Passing – Old vs New School

Passing has changed a lot too. The first change is that every level is passing the puck way harder. Almost as hard as you can. Defense are trained at intercepting passes, so the harder your pass, the more difficult the read for interception becomes.

The old school method was to teach the player to "cradle the egg" which is akin to accepting a pass with a backward flow of the blade as the puck arrives, creating an almost soundless accepted pass. While this might help hand eye coordination, it will definitely not be applied in an actual game.

If you listen carefully to an Elite level hockey game you will hear the snap of the puck arriving on each blade. Teams now snap the puck around and the technology of the stick enables the user to easily accept laser beam passes.

The key to accepting a hard pass without it bobbling on your blade is to accept the pass on the heel side of your blade. Anything towards the middle or toe will pop up and you will lose control briefly. The same goes for the backhand side, try to catch all passes as close to the heel as possible.

It takes some practice, but after you learn this important skill, passing becomes much easier.

5. Cycling – 80's vs today's game

There is really nowhere to start except for "old school" - where a forward skated the puck from the goaline towards his own defense and at some point, "reverses" the puck back down toward his next teammate coming up the wall and it continues. The variation might be it starts lower, closer to the net and stays between the hash marks and the net. It reminds me of a Farris wheel except nobody is having fun.

I have never seen a goal scored using this traditional cycle. I am not sure how this became a part of our hockey lore. Of course it will provide some "puck protection," but other than that, I can't see how cycling is effective at all.

<u>New School</u>

This is way more fun... Replace the old way with a ton of misdirection and with the proper use of fakes (a "random cycle" is extremely dangerous). Players can go in both directions and cutback (tight turns are encouraged), players can give both direct and indirect passes and use scissor plays to drop or fake drop the puck to create off-balance defending.

At higher levels, the defenseman also forms part of the equation, coming off the blueline to add to the scissor effect. This is such a great tool for creating offense. Dmen must veer away from "standing" on the blueline and look for ways to get involved in the offense "away from the blueline." Skating through the slot or down the boards are two ways defensemen can help generate offense. It creates more space up high for the forwards to work and it makes defenders wonder which guy they are supposed to cover!

MK Thoughts

Along with effective scissor plays, players must also learn how to pick (interfere) with defending players, without getting a penalty. These plays mimic "screen" plays by NBA players and "pick and roll" plays. It takes some practice, but when used effectively, scissors plays lead to a lot of offense!

6. Backchecking (now called "Tracking," a Ken Hitchcock term)

Times have changed here too. I was always taught to backcheck and look over my shoulder and pick up the player behind me – unless there was an outnumbered rush in which I tried to catch the "high" player. This was great for the offense because the offensive players had more time to create a play without the nuisance of a backchecker chasing me down. Often good players were able to cut to the middle and dish the puck to an attacking winger. If no defense came to you, great, you could meander towards a shooting area and rip a shot on net with driving players pouncing on rebounds.

Not anymore. Players skate back ferociously. And they attack the puck carrier from behind. This limits the options of the puck handler and efficiently squeezes the offensive player into making plays earlier and often unsuccessfully. It is really hard to make offense happen with somebody back checking right behind you.

For this reason, players see a 3 on 2 rush as a very limited and challenging way to generate a scoring chance. Moreover, in youth hockey, I would suggest that with a back checker the success rate is close to 0% in generating even a quality chance on goal. That is, with a dedicated back checker chasing.

In youth hockey we still see coaches teaching the puck entry to go wide, the middle player to go to the net and the far player to cut into the slot. Try doing this with a back checker! I doubt there is a very good chance that the pass will be accepted and a shot taken. This is rarely used in the NHL or junior and only used when there is a significant spacing between three offensive players and the nearest back checker.

So, instead, these attacks mostly feature TWO players driving towards the net, and the puck carrier is looking for 3 options:

1. Shoot for a rebound;
2. Shoot for a tip by the driving player; and
3. Drive deep and center puck to the top of the crease for any number of problems for the defense. (When making this play, ensure the goalie can't deflect the puck.)

These are the same 3 on 2 entries that youth hockey teams should be working on, veering away from allowing a back checker to turn a 3 on 2 into a 3 on 3.

For forwards to puck handle into a good zone entry position, it is crucial to take middle ice (try to get inside the offside dots) and then accelerate to the boards and drive the defense back. If the defense comes to the puck carrier wide, then a small pass to the middle driving forward should ensue, and the same situation will quickly happen with the other defense closing in on the pass. A quick shot or subsequent pass to your 3 driving teammate should create some chances for your team! For success repetitions must be made with back checkers, (sometimes with the stick upside down) and defense must learn to defend 3 players dead-set on getting the puck to the net.

MK Thoughts

When coaching youth hockey, I would rarely mandate a "high" player in the offensive zone who is charged with "never letting an outnumbered rush" happen against our team. My point is "how do you ever expect to score a goal" if you are continually worried about defending?

7. Offensive Zone Entry – Let's get CREATIVE

I love this part of the game. This is the creative part. How to pull two defenseman together opening up outside lanes, or driving outside and open up a middle lane. How to cross and drop, or fake drop.

Players should be practicing these plays every day. And they need to be practicing in similar situations as a game – namely with a backchecker on the way.

The backchecker has dramatically changed the way these outnumbered rushes work and most coaches don't really realize this. Forwards are now trained from Squirt/Atom to backcheck HARD. And what that effectively does is limit the time and space an outnumbered attack (3 on 2) has to work with. The conventional play on a 3 on 2 involves the following – player with puck drives outside/wide, middle player drives to the crease and the far winger comes across to accept a pass in the middle of the slot for a shot on goal. This is a really old tactic. And it is extremely ineffective because the relentless backchecker has taken up the responsibility to catch the player in the slot.

The new style is to have BOTH attacking players without the puck drive to the net. The outside player with the puck has 3 options: 1. Shot on net, timing is the most important. Shoot too early and the rebound will be steered to the corner, shoot at precisely when the 2 forwards are arriving at the net -> equals a scrum for a rebound or tip which usually leads to a brief moment when the 2 attackers hold an advantage on the 1 defender and the goalie – effectively a 2 on 1 for one second. (The other defenseman usually challenges the shooter and retreats after the shot is taken. Play number 2 is to slip the puck to the player driving the middle lane. Depending on which way this player shoots, it can definitely improve your chances. If a right handed shot player is entering the zone on the right wing and a right handed player is driving the middle, the pass can be slipped through the defenders' triangle and onto the middle driving player's backhand. Once accepted, the puck can be positioned in a protected place from the other defender, allowing a decent shot on goal or potential pass to the other driving player!

The third option is to time the pass to be deflected by one of the driving players. Velocity and timing are paramount, but when done just outside the reach of a goaltender, the tip/deflection creates excellent scoring opportunities.

8. Conditioning – get it done <u>DURING</u> practice

Simply put conditioning is essential to hockey. And if you are a good coach and well prepared, you should NEVER need to condition your team with "conditioning skates." This applies to mites and novice all the way to the NHL. Practices need game speed and game length shifts in drills. Some drills should incorporate stopwatches – 45 seconds or even longer for conditioning.

Coaches should be cognizant of their practice plans and ensure that conditioning is a part of the plan. For youth hockey, one of the very biggest reasons we should not condition them by "bag skates" is the simple fact that you can do this off the ice. Utilize the ice and its value to teach the game and the skills.

MK Thoughts

As coach of a Bantam AAA team, we entered a tournament on Memorial Day. It was a new team for me, and I was excited to see if I could get the MOST out of the boys and see what happens. We got off to a great start, almost pulling off a massive upset to a team that had been together for years – we had only 2 practices. But the success of nearly winning against a prized team went to the boys' heads. So in game 2, we thought we were better than we were and we came out without the same rambunctious, ENERGIZED attitude that worked well for us. I called a timeout, tried to spark the team, yet we could not match the effort of the first game.

When this happens to coaches, I want you first to look at yourself. Was there anything you could have done differently to inspire a better effort? Secondly, I want you to think of yourself as PART of the team. Never think, "they" didn't work hard. Think, "we" didn't work hard. If you continue to see yourself as a part of the team, the respect will climb to unlimited heights.

Anyway, after the game, I told all the players to put on their workout gear that we use to warm-up before the game, put your gear in the hallway and follow me. We went out the back door, and I never spoke a word to them and started running in my dress pants, dress shoes, and tie. They followed. We stopped 15 minutes later (I needed a rest!) and we had a team meeting at an intersection of two major roads. And this is what I said, "if you don't want to work on the ice, then we will work off the ice. Does everyone understand?" They all replied "yes." And then I said, "I better be the last one back to the rink." I did beat about half the team, but that is irrelevant. We rolled into the rink, sweating, my shirt was soaked and my tie was in my pocket, and the parents wondered where the heck we had been. I told the boys to tell their parents on their own, and I left.

Guess what, the effort that evening (even with a 30-minute run) was incredible. Moreover, our team bonded on respect. And what more can a coach ask for? Did we win the tournament? HK.

You cannot expect a high level of buy-in if the individuals do not feel the ownership of the vision. Setting goals is an effective way to communicate your vision to the team.

The goals I'm more interested in are the ones the athlete controls or process goals as opposed to result goals. For example, if a player says his goal is to score 20 goals then I want to see what he is going to do to achieve that. Is he shooting 50 bucks every day after practice focusing on hitting the net?

9. Skill Building

The way to put skill drills to proper use is to build up the way we do the skill. Let's continue to take the toe drag as an example. Let's first talk about reaching the puck out toward the defender and the idea is to coerce the defender to take a stab at poking the puck away. To do this effectively, you have to bring your hands closer together, reaching the puck out. To do this I would have players stand stationary and practice reaching the puck out away from their body and then quickly moving the puck back towards their body. There are two types of toe drags. First, and the simpler one employed by Jordan Eberle, is using the backhand side of the stick to bring the puck back to the body, flipping the stick ahead of the puck and pulling the puck back while sliding the bottom hand back into a normal hand position (one elbow down from the top hand).

Great, so we have a stationary player practicing this move. Then we add in moving the skate (righties, right skate) and make the player pull the puck back towards the body while the right skate pushes back to allow the hips to make room for the hands to get even closer to the body. (The distance the puck moves in this skill is important.)

Then we practice skating slowly and towards a series of cones, reaching the puck ahead of the cone, lowering your back as you do this and then pulling the puck to the hip and clearing the leg away (keeping the toe on the ice – this is why I call this a toe drag, because the toe of your skate drags on the ice).

And finally, we practice moving the puck by pushing the hands back out in front of the body and coming up to the natural skating position. By this time, you are ahead of the cone. And we do this 5 more times going up the ice.

On the way back, we practice making this move against a stationary player who feigns "going" for the puck.

On the way back again, we practice making this move against a moving player (backwards) who also feigns "going for the puck."

MK's Thoughts

Once we are OK at this move, we are ready to try it in practice and once we get to the higher levels we know that this particular move rarely works, as defensemen don't poke at the puck enough to take their balance away and they never look at the puck, which renders this move fairly hopeless! Darryl Belfry will call this move "irrelevant" at the highest level.

The point though is that there must be a series of skills that must be linked together to perform this skill. Then once the athlete can perform the skill once again the tough part takes over from here: The ability to identify "WHEN TO USE THIS SKILL" and as coaches, we must once again be building the "experience bank" so that players can continue to fail and learn. And this is done during game-like practicing.

Skills are enjoyable to learn. Look at video games, for example; kids learn to maneuverer over and over again with failure present every step of the way. But mastery begins to set in with continued attempts – which we call repetitions. Athletes and coaches must understand that skill acquisition is only relevant if the player can access this skill in a game environment. For me personally that means that we need to pressure our athletes into solving and repeating at the same time. The scenario must dictate reaction. And reaction must consist of a vault full of ways to solve.

There is no correct way to pass the puck to a teammate on a 2 on 1. There are a ton of correct ways to do this. And there are even more incorrect or failures that ensue on the journey to success.

Remember, to get the skill acquisition; it must be a part of our problem-solving vault that we can access in micro seconds, and the only way to do this is to have seen and tried to solve through experience. The more experiences we encounter, the more quickly we can find our way to success, and it all comes through – failure.

Some traits of predicting future pros are behavioral. Future pros TRAINED MORE and longed to train and took responsibility for their training. The best athletes are the first players to ask, "why would I do that? Why not do this?"

I hope more coaches can truly understand the RISK associated with each OUTUMBERED attack.

Put two offensive players in a perfect position – say the winger spots of the center ice circle. Put a backchecker on the blueline and a defender on the opposing blueline. On the whistle, the two forwards take a 2 on 1 with a backchecker coming hard. What do you think the conversion rate is for hockey's best-outnumbered situation - a 2 on 1? The answer will blow your mind. For youth hockey, the conversion rate is less than 10%. Way less than 1 out of 10. Once players get to junior, the success rate climbs but is still less than 1 out of 5 = 20%.

Try it. So for the sake of a much less than 10% chance, I am not going to worry if my high forward gets sucked down low – too often. There is merit in teaching that the high guy needs to be responsible; I just don't see the merit in tongue lashing a forward who tries for some offense despite the defensive responsibilities. (If you lose the gamble, I better see the crazy backchecking legs kick into high gear!)

This philosophy changes when "winning" truly matters – basically in the NHL. So, unless you are playing there, I would worry a little less about being "high" in the offensive zone, and worry more about back checking relentlessly when the time comes. Players must focus on scoring goals, and in the offensive zone, players need to have the freedom to move and create without being structured into spots on the ice.

Let's have a look at one piece of data driven by Chris Hall. This is what Chris observed over a weekend of College hockey games in 2015. 12 games played. 66 goals scored. Take away the 9 empty net goals scored – 57 goals scored. 4.75 goals per game, a paltry 2.37 goals scored per team.

Looking more closely, only 40 goals were scored at even strength and 20 came off the rush. 14 came from offensive zone possession.

But here is the doozy stat for you. Of the 20 goals scored that were not off the rush, only 4 goals in 12 games (720 minutes of action) were scored as a direct result of a successful forecheck.

From the 16 remaining goals scored, 13 were scored after a three part sequence – 1. Winning a puck, 2. Subsequently losing possession and 3. Winning it back again.

Goaltenders were beat "clean" by only 15 shots. By "clean," the goalie had a clear view and was set in position to make the save; 15 goals, resulting in a 26% of the total goals scored. 18 goals were the result of a pass. 12 goals were scored on a rebound. And 12 goals were scored with traffic at the net, tips and screens.

What to take away from this? First, we have to spend a lot more time teaching players how to score goals than we do to defend them. Second, it is clear that dumping pucks is a sure fire way to kill time on the clock and the expectation of scoring should be dramatically reduced.

If this is the case – how can we teach players to make more creative plays in the Neutral Zone?! This would be akin to "losing my mind" for an old school coach. A turnover? In the neutral zone? When we could have gotten the puck deep? Yep, that is the normal response.

What we don't hear about is a coach who is constantly teaching how to create offense from the neutral zone, how to separate speedy players to attack defensemen who have had their backward speed matching abilities stripped from them because of a backward pass. How to add a defenseman into the army of attacking players? All of these techniques are new school and if you watch closely, you see them in a lot of NHL hockey games.

2. Effective Decision-Making

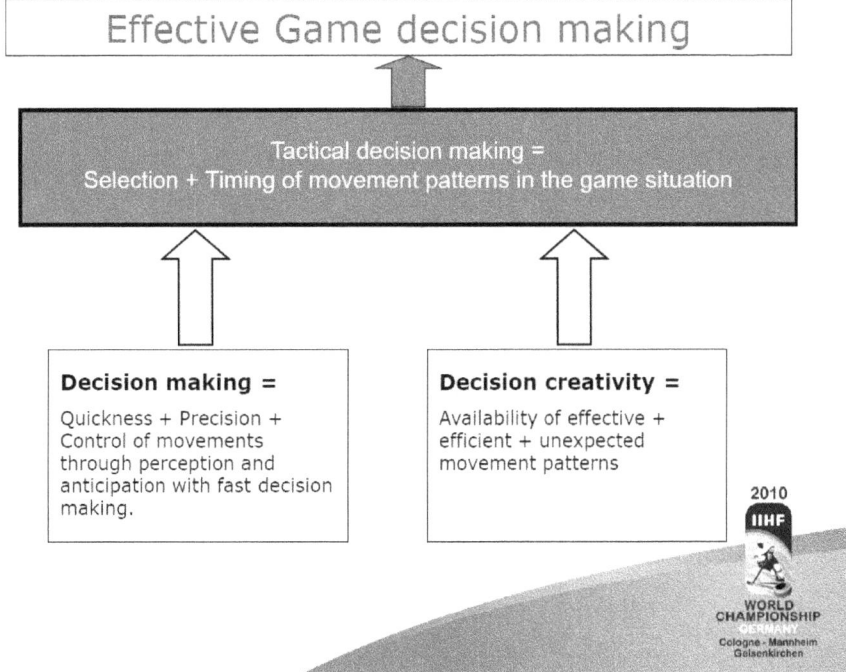

As a coach, if you dive deeper and decide for yourself that this is extremely important, then you have to figure out "HOW?" – to get players make DECISIONS.

The answer lies in practice. A deliberate practice. A practice that specializes in enhancing the decision making process. Throw away your drill book. Shape the environment. Write a practice plan then ask yourself – how many decisions are my players making today? If they are making a lot – perfect, if not

– how can I add some component into my plan where "thought" is a crucial piece of the plan?

If we go back to the story about the chess pieces and a grandmaster vs. a club level player – we know that they both possess the same memory recall. However, a grandmaster can chunk patterns together. So the way this applies to youth hockey is that we have to put players into situations that are game-like so that when they solve the problem, the players chunk together similar patterns to identify a probable solution. This IMPROVES decision-making skills and actually forms decision habit skills.

Hockey is full of situations that resemble each other. Faceoffs. Forechecks. Breakouts. The game is full of them. But what we need to look at is that the situation must be able to be computed by the player. Easy for a faceoff, much tougher for a won puck battle down low. What are my options? What is the best way to solve this – how do I create a scoring chance? How do I use my teammates? If my teammate and I are on the same page, how can we manipulate the defense to gain an advantage?

Factors influencing quick decision making

- Perception speed → Information retention
- Anticipation speed → Prognosis ability
- Decision speed → Decision processes
- Reaction speed → Initialization processes
- Movement speed → Quickness without the Puck
- Action speed → Quickness with the Puck

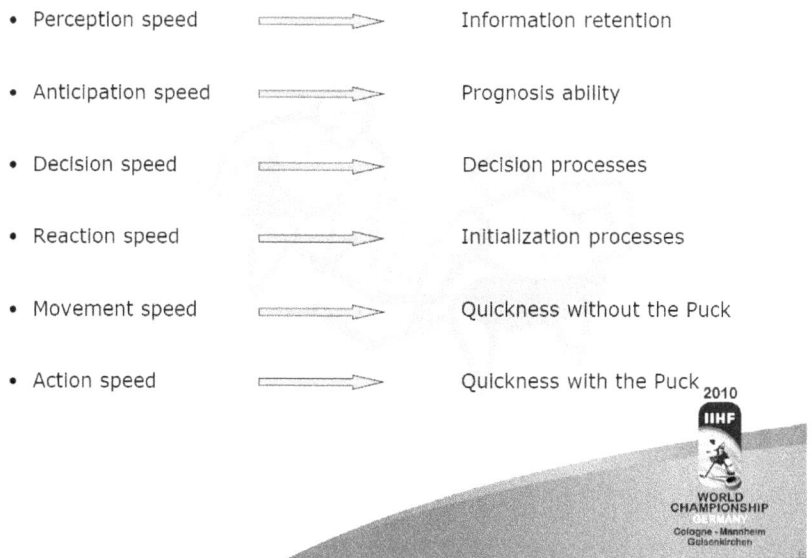

The above chart makes a lot of sense. Now the job of a coach is to consistently put our players in positions to improve these skills. React. Anticipate. Good stuff here. What we need to stop doing is, "defense break the team out with a reverse to your partner, to wing to center." How does that help anybody? Send in the forecheck. Turn the sticks upside down. Urge random movements. Urge players to solve problems; which is another way to say, "practice your skills to overcome the problem" rather than moving your problem on to the next player.

Conditions for achievement of quick decisions

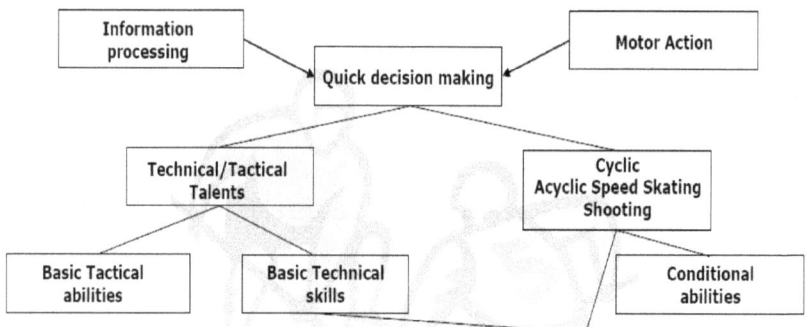

There is too much information on this chart for me personally, but the one key concept is the technical / tactical skills. Obviously we can't expect a player to solve a complex equation without first having the basic ability. If you can skate well enough, tight turn for example, it might be too difficult to technically perform the answer to the problem.

However, I think this point is fairly moot – as long as our team's skill level is fairly consistent across the board, the tactical ability should be complimented with the technical ability to solve problems. For teams that have a broader array of skill sets, it is encouraged to keep the more skilled players together and the less skilled players together so that each group has the same success to failure ratios.

Time-Frames in decision making

Information-taken in = Perception	Data processing (Interpretation, Decision)	Motor Execution = Action
	Thinking process	**Quality**
X 0,1s	X 0,15 – 0,25s	X 0,15s

Signal / Signal perceived — Conclusion of action

Investing in quicker and better decision making is very worthwhile!

2010 IIHF WORLD CHAMPIONSHIP GERMANY Cologne - Mannheim Gelsenkirchen

You can see from this chart that time is a factor in managing the skill. Hockey is a fast game at EVERY age level. When players are younger, yes they have more time to make decisions, but they do not have the same CHUNKING experience to rely on to put similar situations together. So, in fact, the game might be faster for them, and when they become older, they can use that past experiences to achieve premium results.

With a fast game comes a fast mind and a fast motor. We as coaches must continue to put players in shaped environments which add to the players' ability to think and react.

3. Best Curriculum & Core Skills

To run an effective association, coaches must agree on a curriculum as approved by the association's board of directors. Simply put, the coaches will no longer be the ones to decide what the curriculum is for each age group.

Instead, coaches will be allowed to divide up the curriculum into the BLOCK training plans. Coaches can decide on when the skills can be addressed, and each coach can build the training blocks for the upcoming season.

The blocks have two key features: first, it keeps the players engaged and learning. Second, it keeps parents on the same page as the coaching staff, allowing more transparency into what exactly is being taught to your players. A refreshing approach!

Last, implementing these Block plans keeps our coaches from getting sidetracked and focuses their attention on the long-term player development. A term we often use but have no idea <u>how</u> to ensure.

Look at the following 5 age appropriate tables:

Mite / Novice / U8   Squirt / Atom / U10

Peewee / U12   Bantam / U14   Midget / U16

U16 Hockey - Core Skills

Faceoff	Moving Passing	Shooting	Other	Other
Specialty faceoffs	Scissor	Slap shot fake with speed	Effective use of skates- interrupt plays	Deflection in motion
6 on 5 - last minute plays	Interference / Screen Scissor	Pull and shoot fake and then shoot	Game Clock management	Quickness
4 on 3 - all over the ice plays	High Roller	Shoot off stickhandle	Change system down by 1 goal	Speed - improve this
5 on 3 - score quickly off faceoff	Activating defense into offense	Release puck quicker	Break the trap	Eye Fakes
				Skate fakes
				Escape moves

Offensive Tactics	Defensive Tactics	Neutral Zone Tactics	Breakout	Power Play / Penalty Kill
Get off boards attack	1 on 2 defending	Counter attacks	Find center on breakout	Change sides
Scissor and explode	Skating forward to eliminate in NZ	Backchecking support	Find stretch pass (breakaway)	Automatic passes when in trouble
Manipulate defenders	Stepping up at blueline or NZ	D2 picking up pucks behind D1	Control Breakout	Soft area slot passes
use of eye, skate and body fakes	PK aggressive on bobbles	PK Step ups	Effective use of glass	One touch passing
Identify dropped sticks		One timer - power and accuracy	NZ hinge	Pass back - PP breakout
Identify weak players		One timer in motion (2 on 1 style)	Weakside D Jump into attack	PK
Push off to get open		Cut fake shot and shoot	High flickers	3 on 5, triangle position, rotate
Find soft scoring areas				Blocking passes with body/arms
Stick position for scoring				Effective use of stick

Emotional	Age Appropriate	Life Skills	Practice Focus	Fitness
PLAY WITH CONFIDENCE	CREATIVE PRACTICES	PREPARATION	50% INDIVIDUAL SKILLS	POWER INCREASE
BALANCE SCHOOL AND HOCKEY	WORK TO REST RATIO	WORK ETHIC	20% SMALL AREA GAMES	INCREASED AEROBIC
EMOTIONAL CHALLENGES	TEAM CONCEPT	PEER PRESSURE	30% TEAM PLAY (SYSTEMS)	SHORTER / FASTER SHIFTS
EMPHASIS ON GAME RESULTS	HOCKEY SENSE	CARE FOR TEAM SUCCESS	DECISIONS BASED DRILLS	HOCKEY SENSE
PRE GAME ROUTINE		PERFORM YOUR BEST	SMALL AREA GAMES	INDIVIDUAL GAME WARMUPS

Random vs Block Drills - am I doing enough Random Drills?	What is the WORK to REST ratio for each player?	What makes an excellent passing drill?	Is this an effective practice?	Failure. Are my defensemen getting beat 50% of the time?

Bantam Hockey - Core Skills

Faceoff	Moving Passing	Shooting	Body checking	Other
Specialty faceoffs	Moving saucer backhand passes	Slap shot with speed	Shoulder Check	Deflection in motion
6 on 5	Stretch pass	Pull and shoot (wrist and slap)	Hip Check	Quickness
4 on 3	Chip pass	Push and shoot	Avoid getting hit	Speed - improve this
5 on 3		Deke and shoot	Reverse hit	Eye Fakes
		One timer		Skate fakes
		One timer in motion		Escape moves
		Out and shoot		

Offensive Tactics	Defensive Tactics	Neutral Zone Tactics	Breakout	Power Play / Penalty Kill
Change point of attack	Winger pinched on	Regroup	Breakout under pressure F1, F2	Attack off half boards
Drop pass open up	Center to support	Forecheck neutral zone	Breakout with pinching	Back door play
Creative cycle, back of net	Use glass, flick out	Role of F1, F2, F3	Talk from goalie	One timers from Diamond
3 on 2 attack for shot and rebound		Defense gap control	Communication from team	Walkout from low position
2 on 2, cross (drop, fake drop)			Unsuccessful	Goal mouth pass
Use point for offense, spread out			Control Breakout	
Effective use of "stopping" to create offense				3 on 5, triangle position, rotate
Stick position for scoring				Blocking passes with body/arms
				Effective use of stick

EMOTIONAL	AGE APPROPRIATE	LIFE SKILLS	PRACTICE FOCUS	FITNESS
PLAY WITH CONFIDENCE	CREATIVE PRACTICES	INTEGRITY	50% INDIVIDUAL SKILLS	QUICKNESS DRILLS
BALANCE SCHOOL AND HOCKEY	WORK TO REST RATIO	RESPONSIBILITY	20% SMALL AREA GAMES	FLEXIBILITY
EMOTIONAL CHALLENGES	TEAM CONCEPT	PEER PRESSURE	30% TEAM PLAY (SYSTEMS)	AEROBIC WORKOUT
EMPHASIS ON GAME RESULTS	HOCKEY SENSE	COMMITMENT	DECISIONS BASED DRILLS	HEAD UP HOCKEY
PRE GAME ROUTINE		PERFORM YOUR BEST	SMALL AREA GAMES	WARMUPS
Random vs Block Drills - am I doing enough Random Drills?	What is the WORK to REST ratio for each player?	What makes an excellent passing drill?	Is this an effective practice?	Failure. Are my defensemen getting beat 50% of the time?

Make Hockey Great Again

Peewee Hockey - Core Skills

Balance and Agility	Starting and Stopping	Skating	Stationary Puck Control	Moving Puck Control
One leg weaving forward	backward two foot stop	Change of pace	Stance, Hand position	Tight Turn w puck
One leg weaving backward	backward one foot power stop	Flat skating	Narrow, Wide control	Moving toe drag side
Pivot at high speed - both ways	inside edge foot stop (gretzky stop)	Control skating	Side Front Side	Moving toe drag front
Tight Turns (360) at high speed		Lateral skating (def on blueline)	Toe drag side	Change of direction
Change of direction			Toe drag front	Backward puck control
				Fakes

Faceoff	Moving Passing	Shooting	Angling / Body Contact	Other
Offside - win / loss	Moving saucer backhand passes	Slap shot / snap shot	Pinning your man	Moving tips
4 on 4	Stretch pass	Defender as screen	Winning puck battles	Moving screens
5 on 4	Chip pass	Pick and screen	Def, invite fwd to outside	Get in lane to block shots
4 on 5	Receiving pass w hand	Wrap around	Pivot the correct way	
	One touch passing	Shoot skating away from net	Delivering body contact	
	Area pass	2 on 1, one timer, stick behind	Receiving body contact	

Offensive Tactics	Defensive Tactics	Neutral Zone Tactics	Breakout	Power Play / Penalty Kill
Low / High Delay	Positioning	Regroup	Reverse	Low option
Walkout	Moving gap control	Forecheck neutral zone	Quick up	High option
Low cycle	Pressure vs contain	Defense hinge	D to D (bank and direct)	Puck movement
Give and go headman	Head on a swivel	Defense backwards skating w puck	Wheel	Screen and deflect
Cross and drop	Backcheck pressure	- draw in offensive players	Get used to pressure	Aggressive vs Passive
D to D, offensive pass	Position when puck: behind net		Defense use escape moves	Active Sticks
Defense pinching	in corner, at point, at hash marks			Diamond vs box
High F3				

FUN	AGE APPROPRIATE	BODY CONTACT	PRACTICE FOCUS	FITNESS
SPORT PSYCHOLOGY	SHORTER INTERVALS	LEGAL BODY CONTACT	60% INDIVIDUAL SKILLS	QUICKNESS DRILLS
BALANCE SCHOOL AND HOCKEY	LOTS OF REPS	PURPOSEFUL CONTACT	20% SMALL AREA GAMES	FLEXIBILITY
TEAM FIRST - NO BULLYING	TEAM CONCEPT	STRONG BASE FOR CONTACT	20% TEAM PLAY (SYSTEMS)	STRENGTH
MISTAKES ARE STILL OK	HOCKEY SENSE	PREPARE FOR BODY CHECKING	DECISIONS BASED DRILLS	AGILITY / BALANCE
UNDERSTAND THE CLOCK			SMALL AREA GAMES	WARMUPS
IN A GAME				

| What is the Work to rest ratio? | Bottom up or TopDown drills / learning situations? | Am I using enough - Game situation drills? | No minute wasted program - does practice start immediately? | |

Squirt Hockey - Core Skills

Balance and Agility	Starting and Stopping	Skating	Stationary Puck Control	Moving Puck Control
One leg weaving forward	Change of pace	Stance, Hand position	Tight Turn w puck
One leg weaving backward	Flat skating	Narrow, Wide control	Moving toe drag side
Pivot at high speed	Control skating	Side Front Side	Moving toe drag front
Tight Turns (360) at high speed	Backward crossover start	Toe drag side	Moving toe drag
Change of direction	Mohawk turn	Toe drag front	Wide puck, drive around defender
	Outside leg stop	Acceleration with power	One hand puck control	Take ice behind defender
	two foot parallel stop		Use lower hand to cut in	
	one leg backward stop			
	two leg backward stop			

Stationary Passing	Moving Passing	Shooting	Angling	Other
Saucer pass forehand	Moving saucer forehand passes	Wrist shot in motion	Poke check	Stationary tips
Saucer pass backhand	Hand passing	Phil Kessel, inside leg shot	Stick check	Screen goalie
Fake pass	Moving bank passes	Fake shot	Body positioning	Block shots
Rim Pass and receive		Fake shot - deke		
Receive pass w skate		Backhand shot		

Offensive Tactics	Defensive Tactics	Faceoffs	Breakout	Power Play / Penalty Kill
Deke through triangle of defender	Escape moves	Techniques	Basic position	Basic setup PP
Inside outside drive wide	Puck retrieval	Def zone loss / win	Support from center	Basic setup PK
Cut to the middle	Direct pass wing	Off zone loss / win	Escape moves	
Give and go out of corner	Direct pass center		- fake rim	
Give and go from behind net	Direct pass D partner		- tight turn	
Role of F1,F2, F3, D1, D2	Cap control			
Triangle offense	Backchecking - track puck			
2 on 1 situations	Protect center of the ice			
1 on 1 situations				

FUN	AGE APPROPRIATE	ACTIVE	STATION BASED	WORDS
WORK ETHIC	SKILL DEVELOPMENT	HOW MANY REPS?	6-10 PLAYERS PER STATION	OFFSIDE
FAILING = LONG TERM SUCCESS	EXECUTION OF SKILL	HOW MANY SHOTS?	6-8 MINUTES PER STATION	UNSPORTSMANLIKE
RESPECT COACHES AND OFFICIALS	TEAM CONCEPT	HOW MUCH REST?	HIGH REPETITION	PENALTIES
KNOW THE RULES			DECISIONS BASED DRILLS	MINOR VS MAJOR
BE ON TIME			SMALL AREA GAMES	WARMUPS

Mite Hockey - Core Skills

Balance and Agility	Starting and Stopping	Skating	Stationary Puck Control	Moving Puck Control
Gliding on one skate around cone	V start	C cuts - left, right alternating	Stance, Hand position	Carry puck - forehand and backhand
Laterall crossover - step and plant	Crossover start	forward stride, proper knee bend	Narrow, Wide control	Carry puck - side front side
Glide turns	Backward C-cut start	C cuts - left, right backwards	Side Front Side	Puck in feet
Tight Turns (360)	Backward crossover start	Glide on one skate backwards	Toe drag side	Head up sculling w puck
Cross overs - fwd and back	Outside leg stop	Backward sculling	Toe drag front	
Pivots bwd to fwd, fwd to bwd	two foot parallel stop		Front to back puck handle	
	one leg backward stop		Diagonal puck handle	
	two leg backward stop			

Stationary Passing	Moving Passing	Shooting	Angling	Other
Stationary forehand pass	Moving forehand pass	Basics of wrist shot	Defend, keep yourself between net and offensive player	Body fakes
Stationary backhand pass	Moving backhand pass	- weight transfer		Head fakes
Stationary bank pass	Lead pass	- puck on heel		Stick fakes
	Pairs passing	- puck no further than back foot		Puck protection
	Pass and follow	Flip / Flick shot		Stick lift
	Give and go	Backhand sweep		
	Moving bank passes			

Offensive Tactics	Defensive Tactics	Goalie	Breakout	Power Play / Penalty Kill
Triangle support	Basic Coverage position	Full time goalie should not be designated, players should focus on skating development, athleticism.	Basic position	
Spread out				

FUN	ENGAGING	ACTIVE	STATION BASED	WORDS
TRY THEIR BEST	SMART DRILLS THAT ARE FUN	NO LINEUPS	6-10 PLAYERS PER STATION	PUCK PURSUIT
MISTAKES ARE OK	LESS TALKING MORE DOING	NO LONG DRILL DESCRIPTIONS	6-8 MINUTES PER STATION	PUCK SUPPORT
RESPECT COACHES AND OFFICIALS			HIGH REPETITION	

4. Player - Self Evaluation

A <u>player self-evaluation form</u> is attached here. Players are asked to determine their own abilities as matched against the best player in that category whom they play against in their respective league. The definition of each skill is addressed below, followed by the player evaluation form.

Definitions of Evaluation Criteria

Skill	All Players
Skating Forward:	stride, balance, speed, acceleration and change of pace
Skating Backward:	stride, balance, speed, acceleration and change of pace
Skating Mobility:	crossovers, tight turns, quick stops, moves right and left equally well
Puck Control:	includes stick handling, passing and receiving
Shooting:	power and accuracy in all the shots, use of variety and knowledge of when to shoot
Passing / Receiving	Accurate hard passes, can take passes in feet and backhand with ease and ability to get head up after taking a pass
Checking:	angles well, completes the checks, checks with intensity
Concentration:	ability to remain intense and stay with the play at all times
Mental Toughness:	sticks to the game plan, stands up to tough situations
Drive:	constant desire to excel in all situations
Hockey Sense:	understanding & adaptation to the play, awareness of the overall play development
Stamina:	ability to play at a high level of intensity through the game & from game to game
Attitude:	unselfish, works hard, listens & tries to perform to best of ability, team player with desire
Coachability:	listens to instruction regarding team play and individual improvement, tries to execute to utmost ability
Habits:	gets adequate sleep, eats, drinks appropriate to remain in top condition
Leadership:	leads by example, cool in tough situations, respected by teammates
Physical Toughness	desires to play physically within the rules of the game, takes a check clears traffic in front of the goal and blocks shots
Block Shots	Willingness to block shots, awareness to hinder opponent from taking a shot, desire to block a shot for team success
Nutrition	Healthy eater, plans ahead, drinks recovery, sleeps enough, understands the role of nutrition towards performance
Overall Fitness	Body size to strength. Can athlete play 4 games in 2 days without tiring out. Ability to play and concentrate when fatigued.
Compete / Drive	Ability to get into and win loose puck battles. Skating hard on the forecheck. Backchecking as hard as possible.

Skill	Defenseman
Playmaking:	uses partner, makes the soft lead pass as well as the firm crisp pass at the right time, passes off a shot, keeps passing, options open, does not telegraph passes, takes check to make the play
Point Play:	reads the play and pinches, supports partner and becomes move involved in the attach at the right time, reads and selects right shooting options, uses body effectively
Net Play:	ties man up without tying up self, protects the goalie, moves the screen from the path of the puck, clears loose pucks without losing possession, uses body effectively
Neutral Zone:	reads the attack and adjusts to various situations, stands up and makes the play at the blue line, uses body effectively, controls the puck and initiates counterattacks
Board Play:	uses body, maintains control or gains possession of the puck, along with boards and in the corners

Skill	Forwards
Break for Openings:	reads play, conserves ice, selects proper path, timing and acceleration to get into the clear
Score Ability	uses good selection of shots, timing, accuracy, concentration and positioning to maximize scoring opportunities
Playmaking:	moves puck at the right moment, gets into the clear after making the pass, does not telegraph play, keeps options open, takes check to make the play, good awareness of all options
Defensive Play:	ability to forecheck, backcheck, kills penalties and plays defensively in the defensive zone.
Face-offs:	ability to win the face-off consistently to both sides as well as a forward and back

Skill	Goaltenders
Reflexes:	quick movements of arms and legs from all positions;
Covers Angles:	moves out at the proper time and in the correct relationship to the puck
Puck Control:	deflects or covers rebounds, passes and freezes the puck when necessary, intercepts passes across the front of the net, poke checks
Lateral Movement	lateral movement; side to side; post to post and protect "five hole"
Agility:	general balance, movements around the goal area, recovery to a balanced stance
Anticipation:	ability to read the development of the play and make appropriate adjustments
Consistency:	ability to perform well throughout a game, as well as from game to game regardless of the score

Make Hockey Great Again

AGE GROUP: Level:

Individual Player Self-Evaluation

Player: _____

Rating Scale

Poor	Weak	Good to Satisfactory	Very Good	Exceptional
1	2 3	4 5 6	7 8	9

All Players

Skating Forward	1 2 3 4 5 6 7 8 9
Skating Backward	1 2 3 4 5 6 7 8 9
Skating Mobility	1 2 3 4 5 6 7 8 9
Puck Control	1 2 3 4 5 6 7 8 9
Shooting	1 2 3 4 5 6 7 8 9
Checking	1 2 3 4 5 6 7 8 9
Mental Toughness	1 2 3 4 5 6 7 8 9
Hockey Sense	1 2 3 4 5 6 7 8 9
Preparation	1 2 3 4 5 6 7 8 9
Passing/Receiving	1 2 3 4 5 6 7 8 9

Intangibles

Stamina	1 2 3 4 5 6 7 8 9
Attitude	1 2 3 4 5 6 7 8 9
Coachability	1 2 3 4 5 6 7 8 9
Habits	1 2 3 4 5 6 7 8 9
Leadership	1 2 3 4 5 6 7 8 9
Physical Willingness	1 2 3 4 5 6 7 8 9
Strength	1 2 3 4 5 6 7 8 9
Overall Fitness	1 2 3 4 5 6 7 8 9
Nutrition	1 2 3 4 5 6 7 8 9
Concentration	1 2 3 4 5 6 7 8 9
Compete/Drive	1 2 3 4 5 6 7 8 9
Block Shots	1 2 3 4 5 6 7 8 9

Defenseman

Moving Puck	1 2 3 4 5 6 7 8 9
Offensive Zone Point Play	1 2 3 4 5 6 7 8 9
Defensive Zone Net Play	1 2 3 4 5 6 7 8 9
Neutral Ice Play	1 2 3 4 5 6 7 8 9
Board Play	1 2 3 4 5 6 7 8 9
Defensive Zone Coverage	1 2 3 4 5 6 7 8 9

Forwards

Break for Openings	1 2 3 4 5 6 7 8 9
Scoring Ability	1 2 3 4 5 6 7 8 9
Moving Puck Playmaking	1 2 3 4 5 6 7 8 9
Defensive Play	1 2 3 4 5 6 7 8 9
Face-offs (Centers)	1 2 3 4 5 6 7 8 9

Goalies

Reflexes	1 2 3 4 5 6 7 8 9
Covers Angles	1 2 3 4 5 6 7 8 9
Control of Puck	1 2 3 4 5 6 7 8 9
Lateral Movement	1 2 3 4 5 6 7 8 9
Agility	1 2 3 4 5 6 7 8 9
Anticipation	1 2 3 4 5 6 7 8 9
Puck Playing	1 2 3 4 5 6 7 8 9
Communication	1 2 3 4 5 6 7 8 9
Consistency	1 2 3 4 5 6 7 8 9
Style	Stand Up Butter Fly

5. "Association" Greatness

<u>Vision</u>

At your Association, your reputation comes down to adopting a growth mind-set. What sets you apart will be your leadership by continually thinking about what you are trying to achieve and your ability to make brave decisions to try something new and even more challenging.

Top Associations have the confidence to interpret research and theory and apply this in a creative, dynamic way. Tradition should be subjected to microscopic analysis and be commonplace at every Association. Why are we doing this?

Your Association must have a commitment to its values which govern the behavior of all those coaching and volunteering. The values of your Association should be felt by every player and parent and go far beyond systems and process.

The Association must have a clear vision and philosophy that has been thoughtfully put in place. Similar to the vision of FC Barcelona – A top Association's vision should be – "think, think, think." "Possess the puck." Keeping the END in mind at all times. Create a comfortable environment to nurture uncomfortable thinking.

The first value that lies at the heart of any great Association is trust. Trust means that something can be relied upon. Surrounding trust are both honesty and respect. A performance

Association will understand that every athlete is treated as a person. Developing and maintaining a culture of trust is vital to the success of youth development. As trust begins to flourish, every person will have the opportunity to take responsibility for their own development.

<u>Coaches</u>

The most sought-after coaches have a very clear vision about what they stand for – what is acceptable and unacceptable. These coaches are guided by their principles and further defined by who they are rather than the skillset they bring; coaches prepared to do the right thing in difficult circumstances, operating ethically and morally.

It has long been acknowledged that high-quality coaching is absolutely necessary to produce elite performers. When a coach at your Association sees their work as encompassing much more than adding skills to the athlete's toolbox, we have a coach that understands the individual and cares deeply about everything they do and say.

Associations need to use professionals to work with and mentor their hockey coaches. A professional is described as someone who, despite having considerable relevant knowledge and understanding of the task, is always seeking new and better ways to operate.

A top Association will pay attention to detail, use careful measurement and integration of science to enhance overall player performance. Top Associations' leadership groups allows them to extract the most useful information and convert it into useable knowledge to guide better coaching. An Association must be driven in its approach to continuously search out new and better ways to help young players and be encouraged to draw any material and ideas from areas outside of hockey. A culture of sharing good practices and challenging each other's coaching approach is a good sign and vital to the success of all athletes, coaches and teams.

There is little doubt that high-quality coaching can improve learning and development.

The aim of a great Association is to identify best practices for youth hockey development worldwide.

The capacity to inspire younger players and to assist development can be seen as something much bigger. The pride of where you came from and the sacrifice to impart some values to younger players is part of the family tradition that must be delicately fostered.

Talent

Talent ID – players who are motivated by intrinsic joy of the sport rather than motives such as winning and trophies.

Champions – identified the following key success factors as being common:

Dedication and persistence

Support of family, friends and coaches

Love of the sport

Competitiveness

Self-motivation

At any great Association, it is understood that talent can be mistaken for early maturation and to compensate for this it understands the importance of persistence and having greater patience towards late developers (as well as the talented, biologically mature players).

The talent of the early achiever can be surpassed by the more persistent and self-motivated improvements of the late developer.

Talent is far from a predictor of future abilities, rather these seven areas of psychological skills elite athletes use to manage their sports performance are a much better predictor of athletic success: adversity, coachability, concentration, confidence, self-motivation, goal setting and mental preparation. Talent is using these seven areas to be able to peak under pressure with freedom from worrying about mistakes.

Attitude is a separator. Attitude often finds itself becoming the difference maker between talented young athletes and athletes who achieve their goals. Keeping an eye on the goal with a long lens.

Development and Psychology

Putting players into calculated trauma situations, for instance, playing with one fewer player, or playing against older players, can start to test the commitment and persistence of young players. Science indicates that elite performers use mental skills more that their less elite counterparts. These elite players are also more skilled at using appropriate coping strategies for dealing with setbacks and the high demands of training.

There are two ways that coaches can affect the psychological well-being of players. First, they can support the player off the field. Coaches are ideally placed given the high level of contact they have, to convey appropriate messages and encourage sound life choices for their players. It is important to maintain levels of confidentiality to keep trust going between the coach and the athlete. To generate higher levels of support, it is important to cultivate a high level of informal communication with the players. For the highest probability of increased player development, coaches and players must make a personal connection. The best coaches understand that their passion for coaching hockey must be equally met with a deep interest in the flourishing of young people outside of the sport.

To achieve the highest player development, great Associations are intent on weaving together coaching passion, knowledge and skills in a way that all learning feels like a personal encounter – one where the player believes and feels that his/her growth and progress is as important to the coach as it is to the player. Once accomplished, the players will develop unshakeable trust in the coach and the sky is the limit for growth.

Second, the coach will have a major role in the player preparation for both training and practice. How do we deal with the pressure and anxiety?

Elite players cope with adverse feelings by using skills that range from goal setting, imagery, self-motivation, focusing and pre-performance routines. The coach becomes a major influencer on how players deal with pressure and anxiety.

Autonomy

Top notch Associations encourage players to grow in pride and the capacity to take greater levels of responsibility for their own actions; helping athletes become more autonomous, self-disciplined and responsible.

Focus needs to be on committing to the broader goal of teaching players to become self-directed and responsible people. Although most parents quite naturally expect their sons/daughters to be successful in hockey, the reality is that a tiny percentage will persist their way through to scholarship and professional opportunities. Given this unfortunate but unavoidable reality, it is very important that all learning the players experience is oriented towards giving them skills and knowledge that can be used throughout their lives. The optimum conditions for this to occur are to be found where an Association's culture is totally oriented towards supporting their players to take personal responsibility for their own learning and progress. With the person being at the front of the culture, Associations must also keep focused that the athlete must be continually educated to understand that it will be by their own efforts and desires that they will be able to meet the standards expected to make it to the next level.

Best Associations will foster a development plan that aims the individual towards negotiating their own plan for improvement, which is a great way of maintaining commitment from players and keeping them focused on their own plan.

Culture of learning

Play – top Associations will always understand that we "play" the game of hockey. And play is a key piece of why we love what we do. An environment where "play" is encouraged is at the top of the focus for player development. When a person "plays," that is when they focus intently on the activity for their OWN sake, they are at play. The person is playing without thinking. New skills begin to show up. Problem solving using past experience becomes fluid.

Top Associations encourage coaches to set up skill based sessions with learning outcomes in mind and then let the session develop, stopping it only occasionally to make a point. Top coaches realize that the game is the teacher and that effort, concentration and persistence forms the main focus for the coach.

Coaches embrace "play" and are confident to fight off the need to interfere at all times. Providing constant feedback is not only unproductive, it is bemoaned by the players.

Parents

Educating parents about different aspects of player development and the challenges they face as they get closer to Jr. hockey is extremely valuable. It is seen as a key method in helping young players to become more self-disciplined, focused and able to accept their responsibilities.

Parents should be routinely invited to meet with coaches and hear how they can enhance the work of developing a young player as a partner. Parents are not a problem and not a solution. They are potential that can make an important contribution to their child's progress.

Practice

75% of training sessions need to be structured as opposed practicing, meaning that players are defending the relevant skill being learned. Spending too much time on technique which is unopposed makes it very difficult to transfer that learning of the technique into a game.

Sessions of training must include some random and variability with less structure by way of typical patterns.

The development focus has traditionally been:

Technique focused – with lots of work with the puck

Then moving towards:

Skill based focus – introducing opposition

Research indicates that moving quickly from the technique focused to the skill based focused is the key to more rapidly transferring the technique into a game. Perfection at the technique stage is NOT required, only the concept is required. Practice of the technique must be moved to the skill based arena that includes opposition.

Every time a technique is employed, a decision has been made – When? Why? These decisions form a major piece of transferring the technique into a game, and the best way to focus on the transfer is to put players into small area games that simulate the game, allowing players to use their perception skills and constantly fire their cognitive abilities. And the best part is that players enjoy the environment that fulfills their development needs.

6. "Executive" Greatness

Be bold.

As I began to write this book, I thought of where my son, Owen, who played most of his youth hockey in the great town of Oakville, ON – the local hockey association could not for one second spend any time on discussing: how to make hockey better AND more appealing AND more exciting to play and coach.

So, I came up with Gold Standard Hockey which is a blueprint of what Executive Leadership teams should spend 50% of their time working on. Follow along and see if you agree!

If you want my help – go to www.goldstandardhockey.com

Game Changing – Executive Evolution

Series #1 – Mission Update – Create New BLUEPRINT

Part #1 - Reflection – Critical Self-Analysis of all processes

- What have we been doing well?
- And what do we struggle with?

There are TWO kinds of Associations – 1) you own the rink and the teams in it or 2) you buy ice time from the rink. For Associations that fall into group number 2, there is no need to look at Bucket #1.

To accurately diagnose a program, we must analyze a number of areas that are essential to running a Gold Standard Hockey Program.

Programming Buckets

In order to have a deep dive of your programming have a look at the following 4 Program Buckets.

Program Bucket #1 – Learn to Skate

- Where do the kids come from? We take this for granted. We hardly know our customers. How do we change this?
- Who is in charge of executing this program and reporting on the development and graduation of players to the next level?
- Why did they decide to learn to skate? How do WE follow their progress? How do we make it easy to sign up again? How do we make kids LOVE this class?
- How can I help parents understand the path to playing hockey?
- What do parents need to know at this stage?
- How long until my kid is on a team?
- When will he/she play games?

Program Bucket #2 – Recreational Hockey, draft teams, balancing issues

- Tryouts – evaluations, ranking of players, putting teams together
- Balancing teams – Pre-season round
- Moving players
- ADM / Cross Ice Hockey

- Practice Plans
- Curriculum
- Report cards
- Jerseys and last names
- 2 seasons, rebalance teams again in January
- Playoffs
- Championship game

Program Bucket #3 – Travel/Rep Hockey

- Hire coaches
- Season Plan
- Certify staff and roster
- Tryouts – impartial evaluations
- Cutting players
- Season budget
- Payment plans
- Curriculum
- Training camp
- Season
- Evaluations
- Playoffs
- Coach manual for each age group

Program Bucket #4 – Value per second (I used to use Minutes)

- How many minutes of ice do teams get
- What is the cost of the ice

- What is the cost of the instruction
- What is the cost of the apparel
- How can we get the most value from hockey experience?

Effective Board Meetings.

There are 5 areas of Effective Board meetings that can be adjusted in order to have everyone save time and enjoy the process.

We all know that Board Meetings are dry and in many cases, the Meetings scratch the surface of what could be done to better the game for the kids. 10 Meetings a year, 90 minutes long – 900 minutes of time reviewing potentially the same old stuff. How do we change the Meeting to become "actionable?"

Effective Board Meeting #1 – Agenda and any document must be sent out a week ahead of the Meeting. Board must not wait until the Meeting to comment on items, instead comment online ahead of the meeting.

Effective Board Meeting #2 – Formalities, New Business, and ACCOUNTABILITY TIMELINES

Effective Board Meeting #3 – Limited time, what is the expectation of a Board Member between meetings? Is this a working Board? If so, what are the real expectations in between meetings?

Effective Board Meeting #4 – Minutes and AGM. Set up the recording of minutes to be uploaded to the website. Let members know about the Election and position open for new Board Members to join.

Effective Board Meeting #5 – Committee vs. Board Member. How do we form committees that report to the Board? Non-voting volunteers?

Association Self-Analysis

Every Association has struggled to embrace its self-analysis. Associations must be able to be open and admit its struggles <u>out loud.</u> What do we need help doing? Technology. Most of the answers to any difficulty is likely lying right under your nose with a member that specializes in your difficulty. Here are 5 Self-Analysis that will make your Association a lot better!

Self-Analysis #1 – Communication with our members – how do we do this?

Self-Analysis #2 – Listening Skills – How do we accept feedback?

Self-Analysis #3 – Implement new programs /initiatives– how do we do this?

Self-Analysis #4 – how do we find good coaches, train coaches and keep coaches – how do we do this? How do we get Coach Feedback?

Self-Analysis #5 – Budget – what are other sports doing? What are our competitors doing? How do we maximize value?

Self-Analysis #6 – What are the biggest struggles of our Board?

Board Buckets – do the job! Or what is the job?

I also put together 5 Buckets for our Board Members to take a deep dive into.

Our Board is comprised of whom? Elected? 501 (c)? For-profit? Many associations have a board that serves to suffice the requirement of the non-profit status that comes along with a 501 3 (c) to match the Canadian Nonprofit Act. Minutes uploaded to website?

Many other associations have an active board that sometimes gets in the way of itself. As a President, you may want to consider writing out the expectations of being on a Board and for that matter, write out the time commitments needed in order to run a successful Board.

Board Bucket #1 – are we running successful Board Meetings?
- How do we run a successful youth Sports Board Meeting?

- Is the purpose more than perfunctory? If so, what is it?

Board Bucket #2 – Do we get caught up in policy....or do we focus on improving hockey?
- How can we tie up the score at every Board Meeting so that for each policy created, we must improve the game for the kids – HOW? Ensure it is enjoyable. Have fun times. Create a love for the sport. It is easy actually.

Board Bucket #3 – (For Non-Profits) By-laws and transparency, the Association belongs to the families. Are we doing the following:
- Ensure that by-laws are accessible (on website)
- Update the by-laws to ensure your philosophy is met
- Do not worry about the numbers, if you get paid then say so, but back it up with accountability to your job
- Do not fear transparency – celebrate it. Open up the books. Who cares? It might be shocking and it might not. Transparency will separate you from your competitors.
- Put Board Meeting minutes in audible form on website – that equals transparency.

Board Bucket #4 – Timelines and accountability
- Table new ideas and timelines for completion
- Progress reports
- Assign people to tasks and upgrade to committee if needed

Board Bucket #5 – Professional help
- Hire someone who can help – from administrative to on-ice
- Pros will be able to share upgrades to the program
- Look at process to see if it meets current technology
- Do we spend enough time and money on "aiming to improve…hockey?"

How do we shift our focus onto the kids?

<u>Action Buckets</u>

Shift the focus on creating and maintaining a better experience for the players. How do we build loyalty to the point where parents want to help? Where parents understand our philosophy and embrace it? How do we communicate what we are doing with our Association?

Action Bucket #1 – How to rate the experience of a new player and new parents? Survey it. Feel it, be there with new parents.

Action Bucket #2 – How do we communicate what we are doing to improve youth hockey? Constant Contact. Website. Posters.

Action Bucket #3 - Where do improvement ideas come from? It usually comes from parents and players, usually not the Board. How do we set ourselves up to listen to the members?

Action Bucket #4 - How do we get more parents involved in our culture and remove them from the gossip columns?

Board Members – short, medium and long term plans

Any good Board will have limits to terms on each member. For good reason, we need to look at how to transition the work previously done to the work currently being done to the work coming in the future. It is essential to have a well thought out 10 year plan. 1 year, 3 year and 5 year plans for what the goals are of the Association.

Timeline Planning #1 – Write out the Plan and set goals for your Association

Timeline Planning #2 – Work towards goals in a project management style system

Timeline Planning #3 – Transition Plan and Goals to newly elected members

What do we waste our time on? Redundancy.

As an Association, what areas do we circle around and waste precious time on? Tournaments? Approval process? Re-creation of last year's program? Budgets? Teaching parents the rules? Setting up Boards on the ice for Mites? Discipline? Referees?

Consider committees that are not Board Members, who instead only report to the Board.

Negotiate.

As an Association, we have size and with size comes strength. How do we leverage our size? Contracts with Power Skating coaches, airline baggage fees, hourly ice costs, etc.? Are we negotiating as well as we could be?

Reserve?

Many associations accumulate reserves. The President must endorse a "policy" that the reserves must not accumulate to an excess of a certain $ amount - at which time if exceeded, the depletion of the reserve shall be funneled directly back to the kid's programs. Guest coaches. Coaching seminars. Better evaluations. Etcetera.

What is the best way to SPEND money on the kids?

Other things to consider:

#1 – Cost to play - $15 per session (60 minutes) rule, market this!

#2 – Why play hockey? The list is long…

#3 – Clinics, stick and puck and extra ice time

#4 – Miles on the skates – what does this mean? No standing around on the ice policy.

I am a believer that excellent coaching paves the way for extraordinary youth development.

How can we spend money to make our coaches better?

How can we incent coaches to want to get better?

Let's not recycle, let's innovate.

About Gold Standard Hockey

www.goldstandardhockey.com

I started this company to have a central place to store my ideas and work on how to arm coaches and associations with a better arsenal to prepare for, start, and finish a hockey season.

I am available to work with Associations that truly want to improve the way we teach hockey.

This site will serve to keep hockey moving forward, and I can't wait to get more associations on board!

Thanks for reading my book!

Mike Kennedy

hash tags #makehockeygreatagain

Twitter – mike_kennedy39

Instagram – instagram.com/goldstandardhockey

Facebook – facebook.com/makehockeygreatagain

LinkedIn – linkedin.com/makehockeygreatagain

www.ingramcontent.com/pod-product-compliance
Lightning Source LLC
Chambersburg PA
CBHW050853160426
43194CB00011B/2132